Information Security Governance

S.H. von Solms · R. von Solms

Information Security Governance

 Springer

S.H. von Solms
University of Johannesburg
South Africa
basievs@uj.ac.za

R. von Solms
Nelson Mandela Metropolitan University
South Africa
rossouw@nmmu.ac.za

ISBN: 978-1-4419-4646-1   e-ISBN: 978-0-387-79984-1
DOI 10.1007/978-0-387-79984-1

Printed on acid-free paper

springer.com

Prologue

This book is based on many years of teaching, research and consultation in the field of Information Security. Between the two of us, we have in excess of 30 years of experience in this field.

During this period, we published and presented many research papers in this field internationally. Both brothers played a significant role in Technical Committee 11 (Information Security) of IFIP, the International Federation for Information Processing, both as Working Group Chairs and as Executive Committee members of TC 11.

We have seen Information Security develop from a purely technical discipline, with responsibility stopping with the technical IT staff, to a discipline which is now internationally accepted as an integral part of good Corporate Governance, with responsibility stopping with the Board members of the company. Furthermore we have experienced the development of the environment from a situation where there were basically no regulatory framework, to an environment where more and more legal and regulatory prescriptions are dictating the implementation and proper handling of Information Security.

All these developments had resulted in the eventual arrival of Information Security Governance, the subject of this book.

As discussed in this book, we see Information Security Governance as the complete environment created and managed to ensure the confidentiality, integrity and availability of the company's information. This include everybody, from the Chairperson of the Board to every end-user.

Again, based on our experience, we know that this book will add value over a wide spectrum of potential users – from Board members who can evaluate their responsibilities in Chapters 1, 2 and 3, to Information Security Managers, IT Managers and CIOs who can use some of the specific guidelines provided, to create a proper Information Security Governance environment.

The book will also be very useful as a text book on both under- and post-graduate level, in both Science and Business courses. We trust that you will find this book very useful.

Both of us also give all the glory to our Lord and Saviour, Jesus Christ, who made all this possible, and who still guides our daily activities.

Johannesburg   S.H. (Basie) von Solms
Port Elizabeth   Rossouw von Solms
May 2008

Abstract

In any company, information has become the lifeblood of the company. In most such companies, if not all, this information is captured, stored, processed and transmitted using IT systems. These systems are continuously exposed to a wide range of threats, which can result in huge risks, eventually compromising the confidentiality, integrity and availability of such information.

The big challenge today is to ensure that a company's electronic information is protected against possible risks which can arise against this information. A wide range of legal and regulatory prescriptions make this challenge even greater.

Information Security is the discipline used to ensure such protection, and Information Security Governance is the complete environment existing in a company to ensure this protection.

Information Security Governance involves all stakeholders in a company, from the Chairman of the Board to the youngest departmental secretary.

This book introduces the concept of Information Security Governance in a non-technical, but very usable way.

The first 3 chapters position Information Security Governance in relation to Corporate Governance and Information Technology Governance, and clearly identify accountability roles. It clearly indicates that Information Security Governance is an integral part of good Corporate Governance, and that the buck for Information Security Governance stops with the Board of the company.

In Chapter 4 a model for Information Security Governance is introduced, based on international best practices. These best practices, COBIT and ISO 27002, and their role in Information Security Governance, are discussed in detail in Chapter 5.

Chapters 6, 7, 8, 9 and 10 discuss each of the components of the model, introduced in Chapter 4, in detail. These components are:

- The Information Security Policy Architecture
- Compliance and Control in Information Security Governance
- Risk Management in Information Security Governance
- Organizing the Information Security function in a company
- Information Security Awareness.

The last chapter, Chapter 11, provides a methodology, based on the full content of the book, to establish a sound Information Security Governance Program in a company.

This book should be very useful for Board members, Executive Management, Business System Owners, CIOs, IT Managers, Information Security Managers, Risk Managers and everyone involved with information security programs in a company.

Contents

Chapter 1
An Introduction to Corporate Governance

1.1 Introduction

Although the purpose of this book is to explain the principles and practices of good Information Security Governance (ISG), it is first essential to define and discuss the concept of Corporate Governance and Information Technology Governance (ITG). This is because ISG has to be positioned within the wider frameworks of both Corporate and ITG.

Therefore, this first chapter will examine Corporate Governance and Chapter 2 will likewise consider ITG. Chapter 3 will then discuss the vital role ISG has to play in organizations and how it fits with these two other concepts.

1.2 Corporate Governance

Corporate Governance relates to the way a company is run and managed in order to ensure its well-being. All of a company's stakeholders are basically players as far as good Corporate Governance is concerned, but the responsibility and accountability for it starts with its Board of Directors and Senior Management.

> Although corporate governance involves many systems and structures, the heart of it lies in the boardroom [1].

In this chapter the concept of Corporate Governance will be introduced, as it plays an integral role in our investigation of ISG.

1.3 What is Corporate Governance?

Corporate Governance can be defined in many ways. One general definition is:

> Corporate Governance can be defined as the system by which corporations are directed and controlled [2].

S.H. von Solms, R. von Solms, *Information Security Governance*,
DOI 10.1007/978-0-387-79984-1_1, © Springer Science+Business Media, LLC 2009

A more specific definition is:

> (Corporate Governance is to) ... establish board responsibilities and demand that board directors exercise due diligence in their roles of setting strategy and ensuring that management implements it [3].

Note the responsibility to 'establish responsibilities' and to 'ensure implementation'. These themes are contained in the following definition, which refers to the actions of 'directing' and 'controlling'.

> Corporate Governance is the set of processes, customs, policies, laws and institutions affecting the way a corporation is directed, administered or controlled [2].

This 'Directing/Controlling' or 'Direct/Control' theme is more apparent in the following definition:

> Corporate Governance is used to monitor whether outcomes are in accordance with plans and to motivate the organization to be more fully informed in order to maintain or alter organizational activity. Corporate Governance is the mechanism by which individuals are motivated to align their actual behaviours with the overall participants [4].

In investigating the general theme in these definitions, the following two concepts emerge every time, although the terminology used is somewhat different in each case:

- Direct, or plan, or establish responsibilities
- Control outcomes, or ensure implementation, or enforce compliance.

This 'Direct/Control' theme is at the heart of Corporate Governance, and is one that will be revisited throughout this book.

1.4 Who are the Players in Corporate Governance?

Before investigating this 'Direct/Control' theme further, it has first to be determined who the relevant players or stakeholders in Corporate Governance are. Basically there are many players, including those working in the company itself, the possible shareholders in the company and the community around the company, etc. However, in looking at the people directly working in the company, it is clear that all active employees are involved – from the board at the top right down to the departmental secretaries.

> Parties involved in corporate governance include the regulatory body (e.g. the Chief Executive Officer, the Board of Directors, Management and shareholders). Other stakeholders who take part include suppliers, employees, creditors, customers and the community at large [2].

It is generally accepted that employees in a company can be divided into three levels, namely:

- The Board of Directors and Executive Management;
- Senior and Middle Management; and,
- Lower Management and Administration.

These levels are sometimes characterized as:

- The Strategic Level;
- The Tactical Level; and,
- The Operational Level.

From the discussion above on who is involved in Corporate Governance, and the fact that this involvement means directing and controlling, the dynamic nature of Corporate Governance can be illustrated as in Fig. 1.1 in the next paragraph.

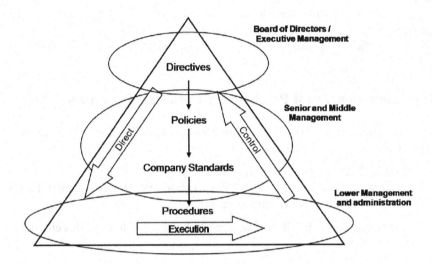

Fig. 1.1 Corporate governance–the direct/control cycle

1.5 The Dynamic Nature of Corporate Governance

This diagram shows the three levels of company employees, as defined above.

The 'down' arrow indicates 'directing' from the top level downwards. This 'directing' takes the form of documents such as:

- Directives;
- Policies;
- Company Standards;
- Procedures, etc.

These documents drive and prescribe the execution of business at the lower levels and were also referred to as 'plans' earlier in this chapter. These will be discussed in more detail in Chapter 6. Note also the 'up' arrow, indicating 'control' from the bottom upwards.

This 'Control' takes the form of control measures, which are the ways in which executive management monitors (and ensures) that the documents setting out the

'Direct' part are actually being complied with. This 'Control' part of the diagram can therefore be seen as compliance monitoring and enforcement.

These two arrows represent the 'Direct' and 'Control' part of Corporate Governance – the 'Direct/Control Cycle'. This cycle represents the dynamic nature of Corporate Governance, and will be discussed in more detail in Chapter 4.

The definition containing the statement "*to monitor whether outcomes are in accordance with plans*" should be clearer now – the outcomes of the plans (the direct part) are monitored to see whether their outcomes are correct (the control part).

In studying any discipline, it is always valuable to identify and study the relevant international Best Practices or guidelines which are available as these provide excellent help and support in implementing the relevant discipline.

1.6 International Best Practices for Corporate Governance

Two very good examples of international best practices for Corporate Governance are:

- The King 2 Report (South Africa) [5].
- The Organization for Economic Co-operation and Development (OECD) Principles of Corporate Governance [6].

These two documents will be discussed in more detail later in this chapter.

1.7 Corporate Governance and Risk Management

Both the documents mentioned above, as well as most other guidelines on Corporate Governance, stress that **Risk Management** is one of the major responsibilities of Corporate Governance. Specifically, King 2 pays special attention to this aspect.

The IT Governance Institutes states:

Enterprise (Corporate) Governance is a set of responsibilities and practices exercised by the Board and Executive Management with the goal of providing strategic direction, ensuring that objectives are achieved, **ascertaining that risks are managed appropriately** and verifying that the enterprise's resources are used responsibly [7].

The King 2 document states:

Risk Management

- **Responsibility**

  o The Board is responsible for the total process of Risk Management, as well as for forming its own opinion on the effectiveness of the process. Management is accountable to the Board for designing, implementing and monitoring the process of Risk Management and integrating it into the day-to-day activities of the company.

o The Board should set the risk strategy policies in liaison with the Executive Directors and Senior Management. These policies should be clearly communicated to all employees to ensure that the risk strategy is incorporated into the language and culture of the company.

o The Board must decide the company's appetite or tolerance for risk – which risks it will take and which it will not take in the pursuit of its goals and objectives. The Board has the responsibility to ensure that the company has implemented an effective ongoing process to identify risk, to measure its potential impact against a broad set of assumptions, and then to activate what is necessary to proactively manage these risks.

o The Board should make use of generally recognised Risk Management and internal control models and frameworks in order to maintain a sound system of Risk Management and internal control to provide reasonable assurance regarding the achievement of organizational objectives with respect to:

- effectiveness and efficiency of operations;
- safeguarding of the company's assets (including information);
- compliance with applicable laws, regulations and supervisory requirements;
- supporting business sustainability under normal as well as adverse operating conditions;
- reliability of reporting; and,
- behaving responsibly towards all stakeholders.

o The Board is responsible for ensuring that a systematic, documented assessment of the processes and outcomes surrounding key risks is undertaken, at least annually, for the purpose of making its public statement on risk management. It should, at appropriately considered intervals, receive and review reports on the Risk Management process in the company. This risk assessment should address the company's exposure to at least the following:

- physical and operational risks;
- human resource risks;
- technology risks;
- business continuity and disaster recovery;
- credit and market risks; and
- compliance risks.

(with permission of the Institute of Directors, South Africa, www.iodsa.co.za)

The OECD document [6] states:

The board should fulfill certain key functions, including:
  Reviewing and guiding corporate strategy, major plans of action, risk policy, annual budgets and business plans; setting performance objectives; monitoring implementation and corporate performance; and overseeing major capital expenditures, acquisitions and divestitures.

As a result of the emphasis good Corporate Governance places on Risk Management, it is essential for companies to have some type of Corporate Risk policy setting out how all types of risk should be treated. Such a policy would involve specifying the types and degree of risk that a company is willing to accept in pursuit of its goals – thus, it is a crucial guideline for the people that must manage risks to meet the company's desired risk profile.

Within a company, there are many types of risks to be managed, including financial risks, human resource risks etc.

However, one of the most important risks or types of risks to be managed, are those related to the use of Information Technology (IT) based infrastructures like data networks, databases, etc. These infrastructures often handle all the electronic assets of the company, which form its life blood. In many cases, if not all, if a company happened to lose its IT infrastructure, it could come to a standstill. In the King 2 section mentioned above, Technology risks are specifically highlighted.

Accountability for Corporate Governance rests with the Board of Directors and Executive Management of a company, and therefore, based on the reasoning above, they are also accountable and responsible for understanding and managing IT-related risks.

1.8 The Components of Corporate Governance

If the main purpose of Corporate Governance is to ensure the well-being of the company, then it must consist of different components, each covering some part of that well-being. It can therefore be assumed that Corporate Governance consists of a number of 'sub-governances', for example:

- Financial Governance to manage the financial environment and its related risks.
- Human Resource Governance to manage the HR environment and its related risks.
- ITG to manage the IT environment and its related risks.

Figure 1.2 below illustrates this relationship.

Before investigating the way IT-related risks should be managed, it is necessary to investigate the concept of ITG further. This will be done in Chapter 2.

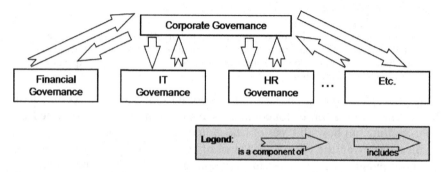

Fig. 1.2 Corporate governance sub-divided

1.9 Summary

This chapter introduced and investigated the concept of Corporate Governance, established that it is the responsibility of the Board and Senior Management, and that it has a great deal to do with Risk Management. Some international Best Practices for Corporate Governance were also identified. In the next chapter, one of the identified components of Corporate Governance, namely ITG, will be investigated in more detail.

References

1. Bollard (2003) Corporate Governance in the Financial Sector. Available from http://www. rbnz.govt.nz/speeches/0132484.html. Accessed 2 April 2008
2. Wikipedia Corporate Governance. Available from http://en.wikipedia.org/wiki/Corporate_ governance. Accessed 2 April 2008
3. Ioannis Chalaris et al. (2005) IT Governance: The Safe Way to Effective and Efficient Governance. E-Journal of Science and Technology, 1, 59–63. **Available from** http://e-jst. teiath.gr/eng/halaris.pdf. Access 21 March 2008
4. Avijit Sikder Corporate Governance. http://www.asikder.com/documents/Corporate%20 Governance.doc. Accessed 21 March 2008
5. King 2 (2002) Report on Corporate Governance. Available from the Institute of Directors, Johannesburg, South Africa, http://www.iodsa.co.za
6. OECD (2004) Principles of Corporate Governance. Available from the OECD, http:// www.oecd.org
7. Board Briefing on IT Governance (2003). 2nd Edition. IT Governance Institute. Available from ISACA http://www.isaca.org

Chapter 2
Information Technology Governance

2.1 Introduction

In Chapter 1 the concept of Corporate Governance was introduced, and it was indicated that Information Technology Governance (ITG) is a very important component or subset of Corporate Governance. In this chapter ITG will be investigated in more detail.

2.2 What is IT Governance?

There are many definitions of ITG, and the following one represents the view of the authors of this book:

> ITG is the responsibility of the Board of Directors and Executive Management. It is an integral part of enterprise (corporate) Governance and consists of the leadership and organisational structures and processes that ensure that the organisation's IT sustains and extends the organisation's strategies and objectives [1].

From the quote above, it is clear that accountability and responsibility for IT Governance rests with the Board of Directors and Executive Management. The following quote gives an idea of this responsibility:

> The Board of Directors of my company is well aware of its role to oversee the company's organizational strategies, structures, staff and standards. However, as President of the company, it is my responsibility to ensure that they extend that oversight to the company's IT as well. In today's economy, and with reliance on IT for competitive advantage, we simply cannot afford to apply to our IT anything less than the level of commitment we apply to overall governance [1].

2.3 IT Governance and Risks

As indicated in the previous chapter, the idea of risk and Risk Management is core to Corporate Governance. Because the use of any IT-based system causes serious risks to a company, the responsibility to manage risks caused by the use of IT is core also to ITG.

S.H. von Solms, R. von Solms, *Information Security Governance*,
DOI 10.1007/978-0-387-79984-1_2, © Springer Science+Business Media, LLC 2009

It is, therefore, important to review the reason why managing IT risks is so important, because that is one of the most important components of ITG.

When a company uses an IT system, the system becomes the environment which houses and stores most, if not all, of the company's electronic assets. These electronic assets include:

- all the data and information stored electronically in files and databases;
- all the data and information transmitted over networks;
- all the system and application software required to store, transmit and process that data and information.

There are many threats against these electronic assets, but some of the most important ones are related to compromising the confidentiality, integrity and availability (CIA) of these electronic resources. It is, therefore, extremely important to always ensure the CIA of these electronic resources.

- Ensuring the confidentiality (privacy) means that only authorized people may read (get access to) the electronic assets.
- Ensuring the integrity means that only authorized people may make changes to the electronic assets.
- Ensuring the availability means that the electronic assets must be available to authorized users when required.

There is constantly an avalanche of threats trying to compromise the CIA of these electronic assets. These come from a wide spectrum of threat sources, including:

- external attacks like malicious attacks from the Internet via viruses, malware, etc;
- internal attacks from disgruntled employees;
- internal attacks from errors made by employees;
- physical attacks like theft, fire, etc.

If these threats and attacks are realized, they can cause serious risks to the electronic assets, and can potentially cripple a company.

Good ITG must ensure that countermeasures or asset protection mechanisms are in place to prevent these threats and attacks from becoming a reality, or at least limiting their impact. Figure 2.1 illustrates this 'Risk/Threat Model'.

Figure 2.1 clearly illustrates how the asset protection mechanisms protect information assets against the risks arising from threats against them. As stated previously, Chapter 8 is fully dedicated to the aspect of risk.

The following highlights the relationship between Corporate Governance, ITG and Risk Management:

> The protection of information can be achieved only through effective management and assured only through effective Board oversight [2].

The IT Governance Institute (ITGI) emphasizes this aspect as follows:

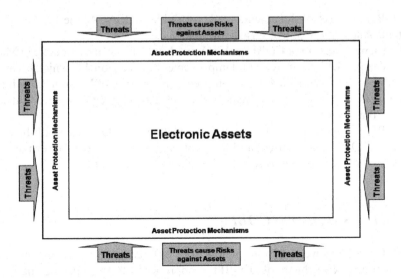

Fig. 2.1 The risk/threat model

> The ITGI recommends that Boards review the Risk Management approach for the most important IT-related risks on a regular basis – at least annually. Boards should be aware of any significant unmitigated ICT risks [3].

A document from Deloitte also highlights the relationship between Corporate Governance and Risk Management:

> Effective (information) Risk Management is one of the cornerstones of corporate governance [4].

The management of risks against the company's electronic information assets is a cornerstone of ITG, ensuring that the strategic objectives of the business are not jeopardized by IT failures and/or the compromise of such assets. Risks associated with technology issues are increasingly evident on Board agendas, as the impact on the business of an IT failure can have devastating consequences.

A very good discussion about the relationship between IT use and risks can be found in [3].

As stated in Chapter 1, it is prudent to have knowledge of relevant international Best Practices and guidelines. One such best practice for ITG will now be investigated.

2.4 A Best Practice Guideline for IT Governance

Several guidelines, sometimes called Best Practices, exist for IT Governance, but one of the most widely used is **COBIT** (Control Objectives for Information and Related Technology).

COBIT, is a set of documents made available by ISACA, the Information Systems Audit and Control Association [5].

The newest version of COBIT is Version 4.1, which became available in May 2007. Version 4.1 is an incremental improvement on Version 4.0, which became available in 2006. Version 4.0 is a comprehensive rewrite of Version 3.0, which had been in existence for many years and which is being used in many countries all over the world.

COBIT is seen as a good Best Practice guideline for ITG. Because of the way in which COBIT was drafted, and has evolved over time, it can be seen as the 'consensus of experts', because many people provided input.

2.4.1 The Structure of COBIT

COBIT can be viewed and interpreted from different angles and dimensions. For the purpose of this book, COBIT is approached from a specific angle, as discussed below.

The basic idea behind COBIT, is that COBIT divides ITG into 34 high-level IT processes. The concept, therefore, is that if these 34 processes are managed properly, the relevant risks are mediated, and good ITG is the result.

Each of these 34 high-level processes is again divided into a set of supporting Control Objectives (COs). These COs are the more detailed 'actions' which must be managed to properly manage the relevant high-level process.

2.4.2 The Use of COBIT in a Company

Depending on the viewpoint from which COBIT is introduced in a company, it may be used for different purposes.

a) If COBIT is introduced and viewed from an IT auditing viewpoint, the 34 processes and the relevant COs may be viewed as aspects to be audited. This provides IT auditors with a very structured and formalised way in which to approach an IT audit, based on Best Practices.

   COBIT is presently used very widely in this way and, unfortunately, many people and companies still view COBIT as an auditing tool, because they have only been using it in this way.

b) If COBIT is introduced and viewed as a broader IT Governance tool, then it can be used to determine the 'completeness' of a company's ITG approach.

   A company may decide to see which of the 34 high-level processes are actually being implemented in the company, and who the owners of those processes are. If one or more of these 34 processes are not implemented, it should investigate reasons why it is not, and make the necessary corrections.

In this way, a company can determine if it is doing the 'right things', where the 'right things' are accepted as prescribed by good or Best Practice, in this case, COBIT.

This way of using COBIT, therefore, provides a Best Practice Framework, against which a company can compare its own IT management approach.

c) If COBIT is introduced and viewed from a maturity angle, it can be used to determine how well the company has advanced in its implementation, and how it is progressing maturity wise.

2.4.3 The 34 High-Level Processes of COBIT

The 34 high-level processes are indicated below. These processes are divided into four domains:

- Plan and Organize (PO)
- Acquire and Implement (AI)
- Deliver and Support (DS) and
- Monitor and Evaluate (ME).

a) Domain 1: Plan and Organize with ten processes (PO 1 to PO 10):

PO1	Define a Strategic IT Plan
PO2	Define the Information Architecture
PO3	Determine Technological Direction
PO4	Define the IT Processes, Organization and Relationships
PO5	Manage the IT Investment
PO6	Communicate Management Aims and Direction
PO7	Manage IT Human Resources
PO8	Manage Quality
PO9	Assess and Manage IT Risks
PO10	Manage Projects.

b) Domain 2: Acquire and Implement with seven processes (AI 1 to AI 7):

AI1	Identify Automated Solutions
AI2	Acquire and Maintain Application Software
AI3	Acquire and Maintain Technology Infrastructure
AI4	Enable Operation and Use
AI5	Procure IT Resources
AI6	Manage Changes
AI 7	Install and Accredit Solutions and Changes.

c) Domain 3: Deliver and Support with 13 processes (DS 1 to DS 13):

DS1	Define and Manage Service Levels
DS2	Manage Third-Party Services

DS3   Manage Performance and Capacity
DS4   Ensure Continuous Service
DS5   Ensure Systems Security
DS6   Identify and Allocate Costs
DS7   Educate and Train Users
DS8   Manage Service Desk and Incidents
DS9   Manage the Configuration
DS10   Manage Problems
DS11   Manage Data
DS12   Manage the Physical Environment
DS13   Manage Operations.

d) Domain 4: Monitor and Evaluate with four processes (ME 1 to ME 4):

ME1   Monitor and Evaluate IT Performance
ME2   Monitor and Evaluate Internal Control
ME3   Ensure Compliance with External Requirements
ME4   Provide IT Governance.

These processes will not be discussed in more detail here.

Note the process of DS 5 (Ensure Systems Security). As this is one of the 34 processes defined by COBIT for ITG, it underlines the fact that COBIT sees Information Security as an integral part of ITG. Chapter 5 will specifically return to DS 5 (Ensure Systems Security) and discuss it in more detail.

2.5 The Components of IT Governance

As in the case of Corporate Governance, which consists of a number of components (see Paragraph 1.8), so does IT Governance also consist of a number of sub-components. IT Governance as such can, therefore, again be seen as consisting of other related types of (sub-)governances, for example:

- Performance and Capacity Governance (Management)
- Information Security Governance (ISG)

Figure 2.1 expands on Figure 1.2 to illustrate this fact.

In effect, as seen above, COBIT defines 34 different processes (components) for ITG. According to COBIT, it can therefore, be stated that ITG consists of 34 different types of sub-governances. One of these, DS 5, relates to Information Security, and that is why it will be investigated in more detail in Chapter 5.

Figure 2.2 must, however, be handled with care. From this figure it looks as if ISG is completely contained in ITG. This is, however, not the case, and this will be discussed in much more detail in the next Chapter (see specifically Paragraph 3.8).

As this book is specifically interested in ISG, the next chapter will concentrate on it.

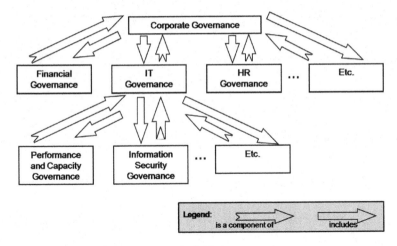

Fig. 2.2 Corporate governance further sub-divided

2.6 Summary

In this chapter ITG was introduced and it was shown how it relates to Corporate Governance. It was also seen that ISG is an important component of ITG.

This book is actually on ISG, and the next chapter will introduce it together with Information Security and also position ISG in relation to ITG and Corporate Governance.

References

1. Board Briefing on IT Governance (2003). 2nd Edition. IT Governance Institute. Available from ISACA www.isaca.org
2. Information Security Management and Assurance – A Call to Action for Corporate Governance (1997). Available from http://www.theiia.org/download.cfm?file = 22398. Accessed 2 April 2008
3. Information Risks: Whose Business are They? (2005). IT Governance Institute. Available from ISACA www.isaca.org
4. Information Security Governance – It's your Responsibility (2005). Available from http://www.deloitte.com/dtt/cda/doc/content/UK_TA_Infosecurity_2005.pdf. Accessed 2 April 2008
5. COBIT (2005). Control Objectives for Information and Related Technology. Available from ISACA. www.isaca.org

Chapter 3
Information Security and Information Security Governance

3.1 Introduction

Chapter 1 introduced Corporate Governance and Chapter 2 investigated Information Technology Governance (ITG) and its relationship with Corporate Governance. It was also indicated that Information Security Governance (ISG) is strongly related to ITG.

This chapter now moves to the real emphasis of this book: Information Security and ISG. It will first investigate Information Security as a discipline, and then look at ISG.

3.2 Information Security as a Multi-Dimensional Discipline

From Best Practice experience in the field of Information Security, it has become clear that it is a multi-dimensional discipline, and these different dimensions cover the span from strategic through tactical to operational aspects.

There is no single silver bullet for Information Security – this means that Information Security can only be successfully and effectively implemented in a company if all the constituting dimensions are implemented in a holistic and comprehensive way.

In this chapter, Information Security as a multi-dimensional discipline will be introduced and several of these dimensions will be discussed in more detail.

It is accepted that Information Security has moved away from its technical image and has a wide range of other facets which must all be considered in creating a secure IT environment.

The purpose of this chapter is to try to investigate these different facets and the way they work together to mediate IT risks and to create a secure IT environment.

The authors prefer to refer to these different facets as dimensions; therefore, Information Security will be presented as a multi-dimensional discipline.

S.H. von Solms, R. von Solms, *Information Security Governance*,
DOI 10.1007/978-0-387-79984-1_3, © Springer Science+Business Media, LLC 2009

The fact will be stressed that if Information Security is not addressed in a holistic and comprehensive way, taking all its dimensions into account, real risks exist preventing a really secure environment.

3.3 The Multi-Dimensional Character of Information Security

The following dimensions of Information Security are clearly identifiable – some come directly from published material, and others come indirectly from speaking to Information Security managers. The list of dimensions below is not necessarily complete, because the dynamic nature of Information Security prevents any such fixed boundaries. Some of the dimensions may overlap in terms of their content. However, the number of and precise content of dimensions are not the most important factors – the fact that there are different dimensions, and that these must work together to create a secure environment, is important.

The following dimensions can be identified without too much difficulty:

- The (Corporate) Governance Dimension
- The Organizational Dimension
- The Management Dimension
- The Policy Dimension
- The Best Practice Dimension
- The Ethical Dimension
- The Certification Dimension
- The Legal Dimension
- The Insurance Dimension
- The Personnel/Human Dimension
- The Awareness Dimension
- The Technical Dimension
- The Measurement/Metrics (Compliance Monitoring/Real Time IT Audit) Dimension
- The Audit Dimension
- The IT Forensics Dimension

In the following sub-paragraphs, a few of these dimensions will be discussed in more detail. Some of these dimensions will be discussed in more detail in later chapters.

3.3.1 The (Corporate) Governance Dimension

Corporate Governance, as introduced in Chapter 1, relates to responsibilities of the Board of Directors and the Executive Management of a company.

> The information possessed by an organization is among its most valuable assets and is critical to its success. The Board of Directors, which is ultimately accountable for the

organization's success, is therefore responsible for the protection of its information. The protection of this information can be achieved only through effective management and assured only through effective Board oversight' [1].

Information Security is a direct corporate governance responsibility and lies squarely on the shoulders of the Board of a company.

The (Corporate) Governance dimension, therefore, has to do with everything concerned with Information Security, and can, therefore, be seen as a 'container' for all the dimensions discussed below. It emphasizes the fact that everybody in the company has an Information Security responsibility – from the Chairperson of the Board to the newest Junior Secretary.

3.3.2 The Risk Management Dimension

Information Security is all about risks against the IT assets of a company as was highlighted in Chapter 2. It is, therefore, important that these risks must be evaluated and countered, just as all other risks to which the company is exposed must be evaluated and countered.

Information Security Risk Management must, therefore, be part of a wider enterprise Risk Management Framework. It cannot be seen as a stand-alone, independent area.

IT Risk Management is the topic of Chapter 8.

3.3.3 The Organizational Dimension

This dimension has to do with the way information security is organized and structured in a company. The importance of this dimension is stressed by several Codes of Best Practice for Information Security Management, which all state that the existence of a proper organizational structure, including some type of Information Security Forum, is essential for successful Information Security implementations. This dimension not only refers to the organizational structure itself, but also to aspects like Information Security-related job responsibilities, communication between Information Security-related roles and the involvement of the Executive Management with Information Security.

This aspect is discussed in more detail in Chapter 9.

3.3.4 The Policy Dimension

Basically, all well-accepted Codes of Best Practice for Information Security Management state that the first aspect which must be in place, before any Information Security implementation can start, is, at least, a Corporate Information Security Policy.

It is very difficult, if not impossible, to start enforcing any Information Security controls if there is not a mandate and reference framework to do so – the Corporate Information Security Policy is that mandate and basic reference framework.

This dimension, of course, also includes all the sub-policies, procedures and standards which govern all relevant actions concerning Information Security.

Chapter 6 is dedicated to this topic.

3.3.5 The Best Practice Dimension

This dimension can be seen as the Information Security 'Wheel', invented, tried and tested by other people. It, therefore, provides an Information Security Manager (ISM) with a reference framework to ensure that he/she 'covers all Information Security bases', and saves him/her the effort of reinventing the Information Security 'Wheel'. Good examples of such Best Practice documents are the ISO 17799, now ISO/IEC 27002, but commonly known as ISO 27002 [2], document – specifically for Information Security, and COBIT [3], as a wider framework of which Information Security is a part.

Although these documents can all be seen as baseline reference frameworks, companies are starting to realize that by following such a good practice, they are addressing most (but not necessarily all) of their 'bread and butter' Information Security risks. Therefore, the relationship between this Best Practice dimension and the Risk Management dimension (see 3.3.2 above) is very important.

Best Practices are the subject of Chapter 5.

3.3.6 The Certification Dimension

Initiated by BS 7799-2, now ISO/IEC 27001, but commonly known as ISO 27001 [4], the idea of Information Security certification is gaining ground internationally.

Driving forces behind Information Security certification are

- to compare the Information Security level of a company with that of a potential e-commerce partner;
- to evaluate the level of Information Security in a specific company;
- to increase customer confidence and trust; and,
- to provide due diligence as far as Information Security is concerned.

The ISO 27002 Code of Practice for Information Security Management is presently the only framework against a formal certification that can be achieved. ISO 27001 provides the specifications, based on ISO 27002, to which a company must conform to have its Information Security Management System formally certified.

Again, Chapter 5 will elaborate on this aspect.

3.3.7 The Ethical Dimension

Although not yet seen as crucial, this dimension of Information Security will get a lot of attention in the coming years, and will be directly linked to the professional status of an Information Security and Information Technology practitioner.

3.3.8 The Legal/Regulatory Dimension

This is the one dimension which is starting to have an immense influence on Information Security, and will continue to do so. Just evaluating the different directives and laws already passed, and under consideration should paint a worrying picture for Executive Managers and Board members of companies.

Examples are the EU Privacy Directive [5], the Sarbanes-Oxley Act [6], HIPAA [7] and the GLBA [8].

The importance of privacy of data will keep this dimension highlighted.

3.3.9 The Insurance Dimension

This dimension is closely related to the certification dimension, in that insurance companies may use Information Security certification as a basis for determining premiums.

3.3.10 The Awareness Dimension

This dimension is attracting a great deal of attention from companies, which have realized that they can spend millions on technology, but if their users/ employees are not Information-Security aware, their technology will not protect them.

The benefit of a well-structured and well-presented Information-Security awareness program for all IT users cannot be overstated.

Chapter 10 expands on this aspect.

3.3.11 The Measurement/Monitoring/Metrics Dimension

This dimension is driven by the fact that in today's real-time, 24×7 world, companies cannot afford anymore not to evaluate their IT risks and levels of Information Security protection measures once a semester or once a quarter through internal audits.

Furthermore, it is no use having an Information Security policy, if it cannot be determined whether the policy is being enforced.

An Information Security policy which is not enforced or complied with is not worth the paper it is written on.

This dimension is more than so-called 'managed Information Security', and includes the measuring and monitoring of other non-technical aspects, for example, the level of Information Security awareness in a company, the responsibility of employees to report and act on incidents, etc. From such a measuring environment, all types of reports are provided which empower all people with Information Security responsibilities to discharge these responsibilities.

This is one of the dimensions of Information Security which will see major developments in terms of products to provide a comprehensive Information Security Management 'dash board'.

Chapter 7 is dedicated to this topic.

3.3.12 The Management Dimension

Information Security Management is a component of ISG – governance is more than management.

This dimension, therefore, has to with the day-to-day management of all aspects inherent in the dimensions mentioned above.

While Governance starts on the Strategic Level, and covers all three levels, Management is on the 'lower' levels: Tactical and Operational (see Paragraph 1.4).

We can say Information Security Management must ensure that all these components mentioned in the definition exist and are effectively implemented and used.

This view of the difference between Governance and Management will be addressed in several places in later chapters.

All the chapters in the rest of this book contain aspects related to this dimension.

3.3.13 The IT Forensics Dimension

This dimension is growing in importance as more and more specialized techniques, procedures and requirements are emerging in the investigation and solving of cyber-crime and cyber-fraud. For example, legal specifications for the way computer hard discs must be quarantined and prepared in order to be used for evidence in court cases are very specific and prescriptive.

3.3.14 The Technical Dimension

This dimension relates to all the technical mechanisms used to implement the necessary protection mechanisms (countermeasures) to counter the risks against the company's assets (see Fig. 2.1). These technical mechanisms are basically implemented to enforce the five Information Security services of:

- Identification and Authentication
- Authorization (Logical Access Control)
- Confidentiality
- Integrity
- Non-Repudiation.

3.4 The Interdependency of the Different Dimensions of Information Security

This paragraph will, very superficially, try to show how these dimensions work together, and why omitting one may cause a gap. Some of these dimensions integrate in a bottom-up way and others in a top-down way.

Some of the dimensions like the Governance, Risk Management and Legal dimensions work from the top down. These are the dimensions with which executive management and Board members must be confronted, showing them that Information Security has a far wider impact than merely a web site being hacked.

Other dimensions, however, mostly work bottom up. However, without the top-down dimensions in place, it is often very difficult to effectively implement and manage the bottom-up dimensions.

Suppose an Information Security Manager, John, installs a lot of technical Information Security measures, like for example, firewalls, and accepts that his environment is secure.

If the firewall is not customized, it does not have any value. This customization must be based on some policy (**Policy Dimension**), which should indicate which services and rights are allowed to be used by which users. John, therefore, quickly realizes he must have some type of policy. He creates the policy, but has no way of ensuring that the policy is enforced. So he creates some measurement system – enter the **Measuring and Monitoring dimension**. He now sits back and relaxes because he has technology, he has a policy to provide a reference framework, and he has a measurement system to inform him about deviations as far as compliance is concerned.

Suddenly he finds out that his measurement system indicates that his policies are not being enforced. He investigates, and finds out that the users do not know about the policy! He now creates an awareness course for users, and exposes the users to their responsibilities when using the system – the **Awareness dimension**.

Surely now everything should be OK. A user phones and enquires where she must report a security incident. Suddenly John realizes that there is no organizational structure through which users can report security-related incidents – enter the **Organizational dimension**.

In this way all the dimensions are interdependent, and ignoring one of them will surely cause risks.

Nothing discussed above is rocket science, or necessarily new – these dimensions of Information Security are general knowledge.

However, in specifically identifying the different dimensions, realizing that each one is important, and taking them into account in securing an environment, only makes it easier to understand the complexities of Information Security and to approach it in a structured way.

Understand that Information Security is a multi-dimensional discipline, and treat it that way!

Also understand that the challenge for the Information Security Manager is to manage Information Security within the context of ISG.

The challenge for the Information Security Manager is now to know what to manage, and how to manage it properly. It is precisely here that the idea of internationally accepted standards and guidelines for Information Security Management become essential for the continued successful career of this Information Security Manager.

These standards and guidelines will be discussed in Chapter 5. The rest of this chapter will concentrate on getting a better understanding of ISG.

3.5 What is Information Security Governance?

Based on the definition of Corporate Governance, Information Security Governance can be defined as the system by which the confidentiality, integrity and availability of the company's electronic assets are maintained.

A more specific description of ISG, may be as follows:

Information Security Governance (ISG) consists of the management commitment and leadership, organizational structures, user awareness and commitment, policies, procedures, processes, technologies and compliance enforcement mechanisms, all working together to ensure that the confidentiality, integrity and availability (CIA) of the company's electronic assets (data, information, software, hardware, people etc) are maintained at all times.

Referring to the different dimensions of Information Security mentioned in the previous paragraph, ISG can be seen as the total 'effort' to let all these dimensions work together to ensure the well-being of the company's electronic resources.

From the discussion above it should be clear that ISG is an integral part of Corporate Governance. The following makes this point even clearer:

Corporate Governance consists of the set of policies and internal controls by which organizations, irrespective of size or form, are directed and managed. Information security governance is a subset of organizations' overall (corporate) governance program [9].

... boards of directors will increasingly be expected to make information security an intrinsic part of governance, preferably integrated with the processes they have in place to govern IT [9].

Chapter 5 onwards will specifically focus on ISG.

ISG must also ensure cost-effectiveness, i.e. a balance must be maintained between the cost of protecting electronic resources and the risks to which these resources are exposed.

Resources should not be over protected, causing money spent unnecessarily, or under protected, causing risk to realize. This balance is very important.

ISG is therefore underpinned by (IT) Risk Governance, in that the ISG must provide protection against those risks which had been determined as potentially having a serious impact on the CIA of the company's electronic resources.

ISG therefore has to ensure that all the elements needed for protecting the electronic assets of the company, against the identified risks, are in place.

Accountability for ISG rests with executive management.

Using the definition of Corporate Governance given in Chapter 1, it can be seen that ISG includes the commitment to establish board responsibilities and demand that board directors exercises due diligence in ensuring that a strategy to protect the confidentiality, integrity and availability (CIA) of the company's electronic assets exists, and that management implements it.

It is interesting to debate why ISG, as one of the components of IT Governance, has such a high level of accountability in a company – a level of accountability which definitely does not hold for all the other components of IT Governance. One of the drivers of this high level of accountability for ISG, is the developments on the legal front. Some of these were mentioned in Paragraph 3.3.8.

3.6 Information Security Management and Information Security Governance

From the discussion above it should be clear that we see ISG as 'more' than Information Security Management (ISM).

ISM happens within ISG, and is, therefore, a part of ISG. ISG starts right at the top, and includes all employees in a company, that is, all employees are part of a sound ISG framework for their company. ISM is the more 'visible' part of ISG, in the sense that ISM must ensure that the policies and procedures are in place and that the operational environment is managed and running smoothly on a day-to-day basis.

This view will become clearer later in this book, especially in Chapter 4 where a model for ISG is introduced.

3.7 Best Practices for Information Security Governance

As mentioned several times before, it is good to know what are the relevant international Best Practices related to the discipline under study. This was also mentioned as one of the dimensions of Information Security. It is always good to leverage the experience of other people as it relates to a specific subject, rather than start from scratch. Such experience and guidelines are usually documented, as referred to as Best Practices.

As mentioned in Paragraph 3.3.5, several such Best Practices exist for Information Security, of which two will be investigated: COBIT and ISO 27002.

Chapter 5 will investigate the concept of Best Practices in more detail.

3.8 Positioning Information Security Governance in Relation to Information Technology and Corporate Governance

Figure 3.1 below can be seen as a sort of summary of Chapters 1, 2 and 3 as far as the relationship between Corporate Governance, IT Governance and ISG is concerned.

The figure clearly indicates that IT Governance and ISG are contained in Corporate Governance, and that ISG is not a proper sub-set of (not fully contained in) IT Governance.

It is the contention of the authors of this book that some of the dimensions of Information Security mentioned in this chapter are not directly part of IT Governance. The part of ISG which falls outside IT Governance is debatable, but that such a part does exist is becoming clearer and clearer. One example is that of the Legal/Regulatory dimension as introduced in Paragraph 3.3.8. That this dimension is an integral part of ISG is clear, but the legal people playing a role here are not IT or technical experts, but professionals from another

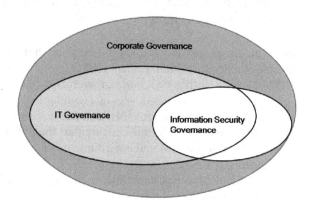

Fig. 3.1 Information security governance positioned

discipline who do not report through the IT line function. The same can probably be said about the people involved with the Organizational, Risk Management and even Forensics dimensions.

Maybe this view can be better formulated by saying that the link between ISG and Corporate Governance does not completely go via IT Governance, but that there are other, maybe more direct links. Chapter 9 may provide more clarity on this view.

3.9 Summary

This chapter introduced Information Security Governance and also positioned it in relation to Corporate Governance and Information Technology Governance.

In the next chapter a model for ISG will be introduced.

References

1. Information Security Management and Assurance – A Call to Action for Corporate Governance (1997). Available from http://www.theiia.org/download.cfm?file = 22398. Accessed 2 April 2008
2. ISO/IEC 27002 (2005). Information Technology – Security Techniques – Code of Practice for Information Security Management. International Organization for Standardization. Available from www.iso.ch
3. COBIT (2005). Control Objectives for Information and Related Technology. Available from ISACA. Available from www.isaca.org
4. ISO/IEC 27001 (2005). Information Technology – Security Techniques – Information Security Management Systems – Requirements, International Organization for Standardization. Available from www.iso.ch
5. EU Privacy Directive 95/46/EC (1995). Available from http://www.cdt.org/privacy/eudirective/EU_Directive_.html. Accessed 21 March 2008
6. The Sarbanes-Oxley Act (2002). Available from http://www.soxlaw.com/. Accessed 21 March 2008
7. HIPAA (1006). The Health Insurance Portability and Accountability Act. Available from http://en.wikipedia.org/wiki/Health_Insurance_Portability_and_Accountability_Act. Accessed 21 March 2008
8. Gramm-Leach-Bliley Act (1999). Available from http://en.wikipedia.org/wiki/Gramm-Leach-Bliley_Act. Accessed 21 March 2008
9. Information Security Governance – A Call to Action (2004). National Cyber Security Summit Task Force. Available from http://www.entrust.com/news/2004/corporategovernancetaskforce.pdf?entsrc = isgfullreport. Accessed on 2 April 2008

Chapter 4
Introducing the Information Security Governance Model

4.1 Introduction

In the previous three chapters, a number of very important aspects were introduced. They were:

- an overview of Corporate Governance:

    It was highlighted that to properly govern any environment, it is essential to provide **direction** in the form of directives, plans and guidance on what must be done, and then also to enforce **control** to ensure that the necessary compliance with such directives, plans and guidance actually takes place. The one cannot exist without the other, and both are needed for proper governance. This is called the **Direct/Control Cycle.**

    Furthermore, the Direct/Control Cycle must take place at all levels of activities in the company – from the top (strategic level) to the bottom (operational level) (see Fig. 1.1).

- an overview of Information Technology Governance (ITG):

    The fact that ITG is a component of Corporate Governance was highlighted.

- an overview of Information Security, Information Security Governance (ISG) and the relationship between Corporate Governance, ITG and ISG:

    This discussion motivated that ISG as well as Information Technology Governance are integral parts of Corporate Governance, meaning that the Board, which, in the last instance, is responsible for Corporate Governance, has a direct responsibility towards and accountability for both ITG and ISG.

Furthermore, it was reasoned that ISG is not a proper subset of ITG. This means that some aspects of ISG fall under ITG, while other aspects fall outside it.

The link between Corporate Governance and ISG does not, therefore, go via ITG totally.

S.H. von Solms, R. von Solms, *Information Security Governance*,
DOI 10.1007/978-0-387-79984-1_4, © Springer Science+Business Media, LLC 2009

Fig. 4.1 The relationship
between corporate
governance, information
technology governance and
information security
governance

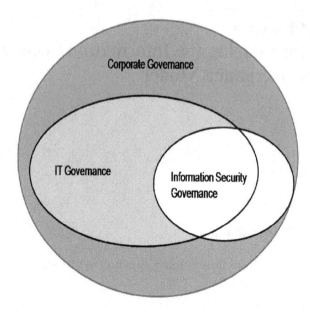

Figure 3.1 in Chapter 3 illustrated these relationships, and is repeated above (Fig 4.1).

In Chapter 9, an organizational structure for ISG will be discussed, and those aspects of it which fall outside ITG will be expanded on. This will provide more clarity on the authors' view that the link between Corporate Governance and ISG does not go via ITG totally and exclusively.

The rest of this chapter introduces the core of the approach that will be taken, and provides a framework for the remainder of this book.

4.2 The Model

In this book, a specific Model for Information Security Governance is introduced, and then used throughout it as a reference framework. The remainder of the book is also structured according to the Model, which then makes the content of the rest of the book easier to follow.

The Model is introduced in the next paragraph, and discussed in more detail in following paragraphs.

The Model, as illustrated in Fig. 4.2, consists of a front dimension (the face) and a number of 'depth' dimensions. Note that the depth dimensions basically only represent some of the dimensions introduced already in Chapter 3. Although the Model should, in principle, cover all such dimensions, only those depicted in Fig. 4.2 are concentrated on.

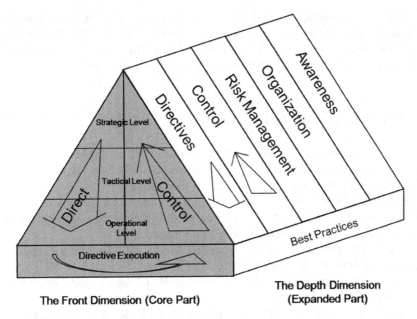

Fig. 4.2 The detailed model [1]

4.3 A Diagrammatic Representation of the Model for Information Security Governance

4.3.1 The Core Part of the Model

The front dimension is referred to as the 'Core' part of the Model. This dimension illustrates the following:

- the three levels of management which are called the:

  o Strategic Level (Board and Executive Management)
  o Tactical Level (Senior and Middle Management)
  o Operational Level (Lower Management and Administration);

- the Direct part of the cycle going from the top to the bottom;
- the Execution part on the lower level where everything is done; and,
- the Control part of the cycle going from the bottom to the top.

The front dimension, therefore, represents the execution of the generic processes and actions as well as the influence of the Direct and Control parts on these processes and actions.

Note that the Direct arrow 'grows' in size from top to bottom, indicating that initial directives from the Strategic Level are expanded and given more content and body in moving down through the Tactical and Operational Levels.

Note also that the Control arrow 'decreases' in size from the bottom to the top, indicating that the number of (Control) reports created on the Operational Level decreases in number as these reports move up through the Tactical Level to the Strategic Level. This will be discussed in more detail later.

4.3.2 The Expanded Part of the Model

The depth dimensions, known as the **'expanded'** part of the Model, provide more detail on aspects of the Core part, and also describe how the Core part is used in several information security-related dimensions.

Notice how 'Best Practices' form a base influencing all the other dimensions. The idea illustrated here is that Best Practice documents provide guidance on how each of the 'top' dimensions must be addressed.

Each of the dimensions of the expanded Model will now form a separate chapter in which that dimension is discussed in detail.

Chapter 5 will start off by introducing some Best Practice guidelines, specifically ISO 27002 and COBIT.

Chapter 6 will discuss the Direct part of the cycle in detail. In this chapter, it will be shown how directives from the Strategic Level are expanded on the Tactical Level to form a Corporate Information Security Policy, and then, again, expanded into detailed issue-specific policies and standards. Each of these documents is then, again, expanded on the Operational Level to administrative and operational procedures.

Chapter 7 will address the Control part of the cycle, and will show how data extracted on the Operational Level is used to compile reports, reflecting levels of compliance and conformance to the necessary policies, standards and procedures.

Chapter 8 will discuss the role that Risk Management plays in all three levels of Management.

Chapter 9 will discuss the way the Information Security functions in a company should be organized to conform to the Model used in this book.

Chapter 10 provides an overview of the requirements, as far as Information Security Awareness is concerned, which should be implemented on all three levels to conform to the Model.

As noted earlier in this chapter, this expanded part does not cover all the dimensions of Information Security introduced in Chapter 3; it only concentrates on a few important ones.

The rest of the chapter discusses this Model in more detail.

4.4 The Core Part of the Model

This paragraph will discuss the Core Model in more detail.

4.4.1 The Core Principles of the Model

The two Core Principles of the Model are:

- The Model covers the three well-known levels of management – Strategic, Tactical and Operational;
- Across these three levels, there are three very distinct 'actions'. These actions are:
  - Direct
  - Execute and
  - Control.

4.4.1.1 Core Principle 1

The Model covers the three well-known levels of management – Strategic, Tactical and Operational.

This Core Principle reflects the reality that ISG involves all levels of activities in a company, right from the top, down to the bottom. The three levels are not clearly delineated – actually they do overlap in most cases. This is normal, and reflects reality.

Although these levels are known by different names, the Model uses Strategic, Tactical and Operational.

The Strategic Level is the highest level where the Board and Executive Management decide 'what' must be done.

The Tactical Level is the middle level, where middle management usually decides 'how' it must be done.

The Operational Level is where things are actually done according to set procedures, guidelines and standards.

4.4.1.2 Core Principle 2

Across these three levels, there are three very distinct 'actions'. These actions are:
- **Direct**
- **Execute and**
- **Control.**

This Core Principle reflects the reality that Information Security Governance consists of:

- a component which clearly directs activities, in the sense that what must be done is very clearly specified through a series of directives. This is indicated by the arrow on the left-hand side pointing downward ('top-down');
- a component where these directives are actually executed, indicated by the 'left-to-right' arrow; and,

- a component where compliance to the execution of the directives is measured, monitored and reported. This is indicated by the arrow on the right-hand side pointing up ('bottom-up').

Note that this Direct/Control Cycle involves all three management levels, indicating that 'Direct' and 'Control' occurs on all of them. This will be discussed in more detail in a later paragraph.

It is actually this second Core Principle which makes the presented Model a 'Governance' Model, and not merely another 'Management' Model for Information Security. (Also see Paragraph 4.5)

These Core Principles will now be discussed in more detail.

4.4.2 The Direct and Control Principle in More Detail

The Direct part of the Direct/Control cycle will be discussed first, and then the Control part of the cycle.

4.4.2.1 Direct

As indicated above, the action of 'Direct' occurs at all three levels. The form that this action takes on in these different levels will now be discussed.

- Strategic Level

    On this level, the Board must clearly indicate how important it sees the information assets of the company, and what part they play in the strategic vision of the company. Therefore, the Board must indicate how important the protection of these assets is to the company. Such decisions are based on several factors (drivers) of which Executive Management must take account. Such factors, which provide the **input** to the relevant directives, include:

    - External factors like legal and regulatory prescriptions and different external risks;
    - Internal factors like the strategic vision of the company, the role of IT in the company, alignment of IT with company strategy, competitiveness, etc.

    The **output** of such deliberations will then be a set of Directives, which will indicate, on a high level, what the Board expects must be done as far as the protection of the company's information assets is concerned.

    These Directives, therefore, reflect the expectations of the Board.

    This output set of Directives now becomes the input to the next level of management.

- Tactical Level

    On this level, the Directives coming from the Board act as **inputs** and are 'expanded' into sets of relevant information security policies, company standards and procedures. Proper alignment of all resultant policies, etc, with the Directives is, of course, paramount.

The **output** from this level must be the set of documents mentioned above.

These policies, procedures and standards now reflect the expectations of middle management of how they want information assets to be protected. These expectations are, of course, more detailed and specific than those provided by the Board's Directives, but mutual alignment is again essential.

- Operational Level

  The **input** to this level is the set of policies, standards and procedures coming from middle management. On this level, these inputs are now again expanded into sets of administrative guidelines and administrative procedures – again totally aligned with the input documents. (In some cases, this final refinement is done on the tactical level). Furthermore, the necessary technical measures to implement the policies, standards and procedures coming from middle management are physically implemented and managed.

  The **output** on this level is, therefore, these low-level administrative documents. These outputs now reflect the operating procedures of precisely how things must be done, and form the basis of execution on the lowest level.

  This is indicated in Fig. 4.3 by the 'Directive Execution' arrow.

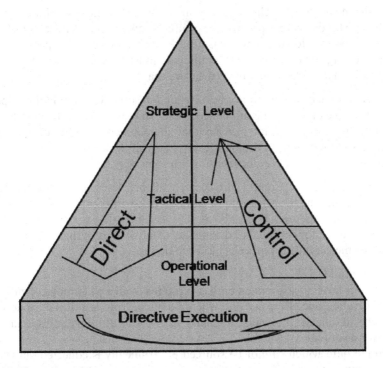

Fig. 4.3 The core model

It has now been shown how the Information Security Governance process is directed right from the top-down to the lowest level. Note that the top-down arrow on the left-hand side, 'grows in size' from the top to the bottom, indicating that directives at the top are short and high level, while 'body' is added on the different levels, forcing the arrow to become 'wider'. This indicates that directives become progressively more detailed and 'populated'.

However, as discussed at the beginning of this book, it is of no use to only 'Direct', if you cannot 'Control', i.e., ensure that conformance and compliance to the relevant forms of directives take place.

This is indicated by the right-hand side arrow pointing up ('bottom-up'), and will be discussed next.

4.4.2.2 Control

It is a cliché to state that 'you can only manage what you can measure'. This cliché is, however, also at the core of this Information Security Governance Model, and is indicated by the right-hand bottom-up arrow. To properly Control (manage), we need to measure, and to measure, we need to know which information and data to collect in order to measure.

This is a very important aspect, and needs further discussion.

The importance of 'measurability' in order to control properly

This 'measurability' characteristic must be at the centre of all directives, policies, standards and procedures produced during the 'Direct' leg of our Model (the top-down arrow). It is no use having a clause in a policy document stating for example, that 'employees must take information security seriously'. How are you going to measure that?

Any statement which cannot be measured in some way should not appear in a directive or policy if compliance to that statement has to be monitored.

It is, therefore, essential to ensure that all documents produced during the top-down 'direct' part of the cycle, must, in principle, be formulated in such a way that the contents can be measured in some way.

As Fig. 4.3 indicates, 'Control' also occurs at all three levels, just as 'Direct' does.

The form that the 'Control' action takes on these different levels will now be discussed. From the discussion above, it is assumed that for everything that needs to be tested for compliance during the 'Control' part of the cycle, the data needed for measurement purposes has been defined.

- Operational Level

  On this level, measurement data is **extracted** from a wide range of entities. This can be done electronically, where possible, from log files of operating systems, databases, firewalls and many other forms of utility and specialized software sources.

  Some data which cannot be sourced electronically is collected via interviews, questionnaires, inspections, etc. Specialized reports can be created on this level using this extracted operational data.

- Tactical Level

  On this level, the operational measurement data is **compiled** and **integrated** to perform measurement and monitoring against the requirements of the relevant policies, procedures and standards.

  Tactical Management **reports**, indicating levels of compliance and conformance, are produced for line and business management on these two levels. (Parts of this may already happen on the Operational Level).

  The measurement data is then **aggregated or abstracted** to perform measurement against the requirements of the Executive Management Directives. Executive Management **reports**, indicating levels of compliance and conformance, are produced.

- Strategic Level

  Reports reflecting compliance and conformance to relevant directives are tendered on this level. Such reports should, therefore, also reflect the relevant risk situations as far as Information Security is concerned.

It has now been seen how the ISG process is controlled by reporting compliance from the bottom upwards.

Note that the bottom-up arrow on the right-hand side, 'decreases in size' from the bottom upwards, indicating that reports at the bottom are more detailed, while reports get less and less detailed as the process moves upwards through the levels. This indicates that reporting becomes progressively less detailed and high leveled.

The rationale behind this abstraction and aggregation while moving to higher levels in the Model is based on the fact that, for example, the Board is not interested in knowing that 321 virus attacks occurred last week and that 27 software patched and 7 anti-virus software updates took place – that is operational data and far too detailed and technical for the Board.

The Board, in order to execute its Corporate Governance responsibility, basically wants to know whether the company's access to the internet causes any unmitigated risks to the company. If not, it is happy; if so, it wants to know about such unmitigated risks.

However, in giving this type of high-level feedback to the Board, the operational data referred to above must be captured on the operational level in order to drive these types of higher-level statements to the Board.

4.5 Revisiting Information Security Governance (ISG) and Information Security Management (ISM)

In the previous chapter it was stated that ISG is 'more than' ISM. In Paragraph 4.4.1 above it was said that it is basically the full Direct-Execute-Control cycle which changes ITM into ISG. By this is meant that the cycle starts at the top and ends at the top – that is Governance. ISM is mostly seen as creating policies, procedures, etc and ensuring that the installed security technology is working properly. It basically never closes the loop to implement and monitor compliance management to all the policies and procedures and reporting back right to the top. In many cases, this is done from time to time by internal IT auditors, but not on a frequent and comprehensive basis.

ISM is very important, but does not encompass all the elements and requirements of ISG – that is why the authors say ISG is more than ISM. This idea will become clearer in the rest of this book.

4.6 Summary

From Chapter 6 onwards, each of the dimensions introduced in the Model will be investigated in more detail. However, before that, the concept of a Best Practice will be examined in more detail.

References

1. Von Solms R, von Solms, SH (2006) Information Security Governance: A Model Based on the Direct–Control Cycle. Computers & Security, *25(6)*, 408–412

Chapter 5
The Use of Best Practice Standards and Guidelines in Information Security Governance

5.1 Introduction

The authors introduced their Model for Information Security Governance (ISG) in Chapter 4. This Model indicated that Best Practices form a 'foundation' on which the other dimensions are placed. The Model is again provided in Fig. 5.1.

In this chapter, this concept of Best Practices will be discussed in more detail, and two leading Best Practices for ISG – the DS 5 Control Objective (Ensure Systems Security) from COBIT and ISO 27002 will be investigated.

The chapter starts by explaining what a Best Practice guideline actually represents.

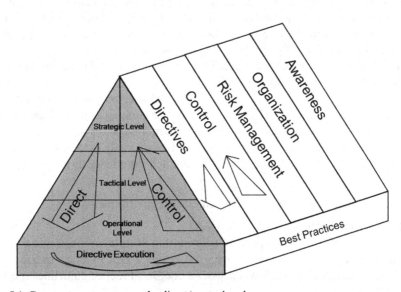

Fig. 5.1 Corporate governance – the direct/control cycle

S.H. von Solms and R. von Solms, *Information Security Governance*,
DOI 10.1007/978-0-387-79984-1_5, © Springer Science+Business Media, LLC 2009

5.2 What is an International Best Practice (Code of Practice) for Information Security Governance?

Such a Code usually documents the knowledge and experience of a group of people (companies) as far as their experience with ISG is concerned. It, therefore, reflects the practices and experiences followed by the relevant people in managing their Information Security

The challenge to any Information Security Manager (ISM) is often to do the right things right. The questions asked by many such Managers are: How do I know what the right things are?' 'If it can be determined what the right things are, how do I know I am doing it right?' These 'right things' are provided by Best Practice guidelines.

Information Security is not a new aspect of IT. Many people and many companies have struggled with Information Security over many years. In this process, they have found out what the right things are, and how to do them right. They have, therefore, determined from experience what Best Practices are required and how to implement them effectively.

This experience has been documented in a wide set of documents, basically referred to as Best Practices or Standards or Guidelines. These documents are available to (new) ISMs, and should be used.

They can be seen as the consensus of experts in the field of Information Security, and generally provide an internationally accepted framework on which to base Information Security Governance and Management.

Nobody needs to re-invent the 'Information Security Governance Wheel'. This wheel has been developed; it is documented and should be used as such.

This does not necessarily mean that if these Best Practices are followed strictly, that no security incidents will occur. That is, of course, not true, but at least an ISM and the Executive Management of companies know that they are proving their due diligence by following the advice of experts.

This approach is based on the concept of 'learning from the Information Security experiences of other people'. The idea is that a large percentage of Information Security threats, resulting risks, and selected countermeasures are the same for all companies. If a large number of companies have documented their experiences in this area, alongside the countermeasures they have selected for the possible risks, why does a comprehensive risk analysis to probably arrive at the same result? Rather, use these documented experience directly.

- Why redo what others have done already?
- Why re-invent the wheel for well-established environments?

Learn from and apply their experience!

The 'bread-and-butter' aspects of Information Security are the same in most IT environments. This is precisely what 'following a Best Practice' means.

The rest of this chapter now discusses some Best Practice guidelines specifically for ISG.

In Chapter 2, COBIT was introduced as a Best Practice guideline for IT Governance, and Chapter 3 referred to ISO 27002 as a Best Practice guideline for ISG.

Initially, COBIT will be investigated in more detail and then, specifically, those Control Objectives (COs) which are related to Information Security.

5.3 Using COBIT as a Framework for Information Security Governance

COBIT, Control Objectives for Information and Related Technology, is a set of documents made available by ISACA, the Information Systems Audit and Control Association. COBIT was introduced in Chapter 2.

As mentioned in Chapter 2, the newest version of COBIT is Version 4.1, which became available in May 2007. Version 4.1 is an incremental improvement to Version 4.0, which became available in 2006.

Version 4.0 is a comprehensive rewrite of Version 3.0, which had been in existence for many years.

COBIT is seen as a good practice for Information Technology Governance (ITG). Because of the way in which COBIT was drafted, and evolved over time, it can be seen as the 'consensus of experts', because many people provided input.

COBIT is not specifically a Best Practice guideline for ISG, but rather for ITG, as was discussed in Chapter 2. However, COBIT has a substantial component related to Information Security, specifically, process DS 5 (Ensure System Security).

5.4 COBIT and Information Security

As stated above, the COBIT DS 5 high-level process of 'Ensuring Systems Security' is the main COBIT driver for Information Security. This paragraph will investigate some of the 11 COs for Information Security within DS 5. Remember, in Paragraph 2.4.1 it was stated that every one of the 34 processes of COBIT is divided into a number of COs.

A few of the 11 COs in DS 5 will be selectively discussed, giving some idea of how they can be used.

The numbering as it appears in the COBIT document is used.

5.4.1 Control Objective DS 5.4 User Account Management

This DCO provides guidelines on User Account Management, and notes some important procedures which should be in place concerning the management of user accounts. The CO requires a proper environment consisting of policies and procedures for accepting new users to logon to an IT system, to grant new access rights to them, to suspend their logons and rights if needed, and to close their accounts when they leave, etc.

Note that for example, it specifies that a formal procedure for granting of access privileges must be operational, and the owner of the specific system to which access is to be granted must be involved. This specification is a good example of the benefit of using such a Best Practice guideline. The ISM might have realized that he/she must implement some type of environment to manage access and access rights, but may not have thought about involving the system owner. This CO clearly indicates that it is important, and will, therefore, guide the Manager to use the advice, which will strengthen the security of the company. The CO does not specify precisely how the procedures should look and how they should be set up. This is left to the company to do, according to its own company standards and approaches; however, that such procedures should exist, and should be used, is the message of CO 5.4

It is now up to the company to implement such procedures.

Using COBIT as a Best Practice for Information Security Governance will, therefore, demand that such procedures be implemented and operationally managed. Note again, that it is not precisely specified **how** this must be done – that is left to the company – but that it **must** be done as part of best practice, is essential.

5.4.2 DS 5.6 Security Incident Handling

This CO advises that potential security incidents, i.e., incidents which may affect the security of the system in any way, should be defined and that all users should be informed about and be aware of precisely what such incidents are, so that they can be avoided, or if they do occur, to know what to do and how to report and manage the relevant incident.

Again, this CO shows that not having such a proper incident managing environment means not following international Best Practices.

5.4.3 DS 5.9 Malicious Software Prevention, Detection and Correction

This CO contains guidance on what must be in place to protect the company's systems from malicious software (malware) like viruses, Trojan horses, spam, spyware, etc.

This CO mandates the existence of:

- a framework of adequate control measures like anti-virus control, to prevent, detect and correct any incidents which may occur as a result of such malware trying to compromise the company's systems and assets.

Again, the CO does not state which anti-virus software must be used, but stresses the fact that such software must be in place.

By following the guidelines of this CO properly, a company would create a good defence against malicious software, and lower the risk that such software may damage the company's systems and electronic assets.

Therefore, to have a sound COBIT-based ISG structure, a company must, at least, conform to the 11 COs of DS 5. If any one of these COs is not implemented for whatever reason, the company must motivate why it has chosen to exclude that specific CO.

As can be seen from the description above, the COs provide guidance on what should be in place to manage the specific high-level process to 'Ensure Systems Security'.

5.5 Other Information Security-Related COBIT High-Level Processes

As stated before, though all the direct information security-related COs are included under 'Ensuring System Security', there are other indirectly Information Security-related COs in some of the other high-level processes of COBIT.

Some examples are:

- The high-level process of DS 4, 'Ensure Continuous Service', which addresses the existence of a proper IT continuity plan, including aspects like back up, recovery, etc. Such a plan should be distributed amongst all role players and tested regularly. This is essential to protect the IT environment against disasters which may occur, which may affect the availability of systems and electronic assets.
- The high level process of PO 2, 'Define the Information Architecture', has, as one of its COs, the requirement for a Data Classification Scheme, requiring that a general classification framework must exist for placing data in information classes, and assigning ownership of such classes, and creating access protection rules for these.

Therefore, although DS 5 is the main process for governing Information Security, there are many other COs which should be taken into account when a comprehensive Information Security plan, based on COBIT, is created.

As stated, COBIT is a Best Practice guideline for ITG, and includes Information Security as part of its specifications.

The next Best Practice document discussed is totally dedicated to Information Security.

5.6 ISO 27002

ISO 27002 [1] is an internationally accepted and recognized Code of Practice for Information Security Management.

It was accepted in 2000 as a standard by the International Organization for Standardization as ISO 17799, but the name changed in 2007 to ISO 27002.

This paragraph will briefly discuss this document, as well as its so-called Part 2.

5.7 The Background of ISO 27002

In the early 1990s, as a response to industry demands for some type of guideline for the management of information security, a working group was created in the UK. This working group consisted of Information Security practitioners from a range of large companies in the UK. The working party produced a document 'A Code of Practice for Information Security Management' in about 1993. This document was accepted in 1995 by the British Standards Institute (BSI) as a standard, named BS 7799.

This quickly became an important document as far as Information Security Management is concerned – initially in the UK, but also in some European countries, and even further afield.

Towards the end of the 1990s, again driven by industry demand, the requirement to formally accredit companies conforming to the specifications of BS 7799, gained momentum.

This resulted in BS 7799: Part 2, which specified the process which must be followed to become formally certified against the original BS 7799.

This resulted in two documents: BS 7799 Part 1, which was the original BS 7799 'A Code of Practice for Information Security Management' document mentioned above, and BS 7799 Part 2, the specification document for formal accreditation against Part 1.

The wider use of BS 7799 Part 1 resulted in the BSI submitting the document to the International Standards Organization. Through a 'fast tracking' process, BS 7799 Part 1 was accepted in 2000 as ISO 17799.

BS 7799 – Part 2 has not been part of this process, and, therefore, Part 2 did not become an ISO standard at that time.

Several countries have accepted ISO 17799 also as national standards. From these, some have also accepted BS 7799 Part 2 as a national standard.

In 2005, ISO 17799 was thoroughly reviewed and is presently the most recent version. In 2007, ISO 17799 became ISO 27002.

During the same time period, BS 7799 Part 2 was also submitted to the International Standards Organization, and was eventually accepted as ISO 27001.

The ISO has decided that all standards related to Information Security will be in their numbering range of ISO 27XXX. ISO 27001 and ISO 27002 are, therefore, the first two standards in this series.

5.8 More About ISO 27002 and ISO 27001

ISO 27002 is a 'guideline' document, and advises companies on what they should have in place as far as their Information Security Management is concerned, in order to follow 'Best Practice'. This, therefore, guides a company to structure its Information Security Management according to the experience of other companies – something like following the consensus of experts or providing a reference framework.

The document can be interpreted in a certain sense as saying: 'This aspect is good to have in place and the company may implement it if they want to'. There is no compulsory enforcement.

The document is rather high level, and does not drill down to very detailed specifics.

ISO 27001, on the other hand, is very specific and strict, and spells out, in detail, what a company must comply with and have in place to be formally certified.

ISO 27001 can be interpreted in a certain sense as saying: 'This aspect is compulsory, and must be implemented – if you do not have it implemented, you cannot be certified'. In reality, the statement above is a little overstated, because if a company can motivate, based on some form of risk assessment, why a specific aspect need not be included, it may be omitted and the company may still get certified.

While a very large number of companies internationally are using ISO 27002 as a general guideline or framework for their Information Security Management, fewer companies have actually taken the second step and had themselves formally certified according to ISO 27001.

A list of companies which are presently formally certified against ISO 27001 may be found at www.17799central.com/cert.htm (as of January 2008).

5.9 The Use of ISO 27002 in a Company

Why should a company decide to accept ISO 27002 as a reference framework for its Information Security Management?

There can, of course, be several reasons. Some of them are discussed in more detail below.

1. Expertise and experience of Information Security Management is at a premium in many companies all over the world. Very often, a person is appointed as an ISM without having a lot of experience in the area. Such a person then has the challenge to place his company's Information Security Management on an acceptable level: but what is an acceptable level?

    Very often such a person does not know what good and proper Information Security entails, and what its management means.

In such a case, ISO 27002 is a perfect place to start. By studying the document, which can be seen as a documentation of the experiences of many people, the newly appointed ISM can immediately get a good handle on Information Security Management.

ISO 27002 gives such an ISM the confidence that he/she is 'covering all bases', and that some very important aspect is not overlooked.

ISO 27002 is an essential document for any (newly appointed) ISM.

2. Very often, an ISM must motivate to Executive Management why certain steps are being taken, and certain control measures implemented. Again, if such steps resulted from using ISO 27002, a very good motivation is always: '.... because we are following international Best Practices and are standardizing on an international standard.'

3. Using ISO 27002 as a standard or framework for Information Security Management, also simplifies IT auditing. If the ISM bases his Information Security plan on ISO 27002, and the internal/external auditors also use ISO 27002 as their auditing framework, it makes life so much simpler – apples are compared with apples, and not with pears.

4. Very often a company wants to get an idea of how good its Information Security implementations are. In such cases, ISO 27002 can be used to do a 'health check' or 'gap analysis', that is, comparing what we have with what international Best Practices advise. After the gap has been determined, a directed project can be started to close the gap or, at least, make it smaller.

This form of standardization, therefore, also ensures a better understanding between the Information Security Management team and the auditors.

Following the guidance of ISO 27002 is also an assurance to Executive Management that the company is really demonstrating due diligence as far as its ISG is concerned, and, therefore, as far as Corporate Governance in general.

5.10 ISO 27002 and Risk Management

It is extremely important to realize that even if a company conforms 100% to ISO 27002, it is not necessarily covering all its Information Security risks.

ISO 27002 must, to a certain extent be viewed as a 'base line' document, that is, it specifies the minimum a company should have in place to have an acceptable Information Security infrastructure. Anything 'below' the specifications of ISO 27002, may be very dangerous if a proper analysis had not been done to deliberately exclude some aspects advised by ISO 27002.

On the other hand, the company may have some very serious IT risks, which are not sufficiently covered by the advised measures in ISO 27002.

It is, therefore, essential that a company must perform its own IT risk analysis to ensure that if it has very serious IT risks, measures over and above that specified by ISO 27002 may have to be implemented.

Paragraph 4 in ISO 27002 (pages 5 and 6) specifically introduces risk assessment and risk treatment.

ISO 27002 should, therefore, be seen as the starting point from where a company begins its Information Security Management effort.

ISO 27002 is an extremely good starting point, but must not be seen as the end-all of Information Security Management.

5.11 The Use of ISO 27001 in a Company

As stated above, a company can use ISO 27002 as a general guideline and reference framework as far as its Information Security Management is concerned, with not too much worry if something is somewhere not exactly as required.

Many companies are doing precisely this, and merely have an 'ISO 27002 Health Check' from time to time to see how well they conform to the Guidelines.

However, other companies want to approach compliance much more formally and, therefore, choose to go the formal certification route.

Reasons for doing this include:

1. To give customers and clients extra assurance about the company's Information Security;
2. To get a competitive advantage against its rivals;
3. To make a managerial statement about its commitment to Information Security;
4. To show due diligence as far as Corporate Governance is concerned;
5. To demand equivalent Information Security commitment from their trading and e-commerce partners.

This last issue is very important, and allows a company to state:

We have proved our commitment and significance to our company's Information Security by becoming formally certified. Before we will allow you as an e-commerce trading partner to access our information systems, first prove your commitment to Information Security to us by also becoming formally certified.

In doing that, Company 1 will ensure that Company 2 does not become a 'back door' into their information systems.

This is a form of Information Security due diligence towards new e-commerce partners.

The certification process will be discussed in more detail later in this chapter.

5.12 The Structure of ISO 27002

ISO 27002 consists of 11 security control clauses, each dedicated to a specific aspect of Information Security in a company. These 11 clauses can also be viewed as 11 'high-level' controls which must be addressed to ensure a secure environment. Each of the 11 clauses consists of a number of main security categories, relevant to the specific clause. There are 39 such main security categories in total.

These 11 clauses are:

- Security Policy
- Organization of Information Security
- Asset Management
- Human Resource Security
- Physical and Environmental Security
- Communications and Operations Management
- Access Control
- Information Systems Acquisition, Development and Maintenance
- Information Security Incident Management
- Business Continuity Management
- Compliance

A more detailed discussion of the contents of ISO 27002 and ISO 27001 will be done in Paragraphs 5.14 and 5.15. The discussion of risk in the ISO 27002 document (pages 5 and 6) is very important. Risk, in general, is discussed in detail in Chapter 8.

5.13 ISO 27002 and COBIT

It is interesting to compare ISO 27002 and COBIT with each other to see how they interlink.

The following aspects are clear from the discussion in previous chapters:

1. COBIT is 'wider' than ISO 27002 as COBIT addresses the whole area of Information Technology, while ISO 27002 only addresses the sub-area of Information Security.

   COBIT, therefore, addresses Information Security as one of its 34 component processes, while ISO 27002 is totally dedicated to Information Security only.
2. COBIT does not have a formal certification component for any of its 34 processes, while ISO 27002, through ISO 27001, has a formal certification route.
3. COBIT is not an official ISO standard, while ISO 27002 is.
4. Because ISO 27002 is totally dedicated to Information Security, it is more detailed than COBIT's Information Security component.

COBIT will, for example, specify that a policy or procedure for some aspect must exist, while ISO 27002 will provide more detail about the content of the specific procedure or policy (see for example 5.1.1 in ISO 27002).

Some people, including the authors, like to see COBIT as the 'what' must be done, while ISO 27002 is more the 'how' it must be done.

COBIT and ISO 27002 are, therefore, not adversaries: they are complementary.

Companies will do well by using COBIT for a wider company IT strategy, while using ISO 27002 to give content to the Information Security sub-strategy following from the higher-level strategy.

The paper 'Information Security Governance: COBIT or ISO 17799 or both?' [2] provides a very good discussion on how COBIT and ISO 27002 (ISO 17799) can co-exist and be used in a complementary mode in a company.

5.14 A More Detailed Look at ISO 27002

All of the 11 clauses mentioned in 5.12 above are divided into a number of main security categories. Each of these categories consists of a control objective stating what is to be achieved in this category, and one or more controls, with implementation guidelines, that can be used in order to achieve the specific control objective of the main security category.

A specific example will be investigated later.

This paragraph will merely list the high-level clauses, the main security categories in each clause, and the control objectives in each main security category, but does not specify the detailed controls and implementation guidance.

For that information, the reader is advised to get a full copy of ISO 27002.

An example of why it is important to have the full copy of ISO 27002 is that in the main security category (11.2 of clause 11), control 11.2.1 on User Registration has a list of ten different implementation guidances which should be included and addressed in a formal User Registration procedure.

5.14.1 The Clause Structure of ISO 27002

The 11 clauses in ISO 27002 are numbered from 5 to 15 in the ISO 27002 document.

The full index of ISO 27002[1] is given below, and then discussed in more detail.

(Extracts from ISO/IEC 27001 and ISO/IEC 27002 appear in accordance with permission granted by the South African Bureau of Standards on behalf of ISO.)

---

[1] ISO and the South African Bureau of Standards accept no liability for any damage whatsoever that may result from the use of this material or the information contained therein, irrespective of the cause and quantum thereof.)

6.2 EXTERNAL PARTIES
6.2.1 Identification of risks related to external parties
6.2.2 Addressing security when dealing with customers
6.2.3 Addressing security in third party agreements

7 ASSET MANAGEMENT

7.1 RESPONSIBILITY FOR ASSETS
7.1.1 Inventory of assets
7.1.2 Ownership of assets
7.1.3 Acceptable use of assets

7.2 INFORMATION CLASSIFICATION
7.2.1 Classification guidelines
7.2.2 Information labeling and handling

8 HUMAN RESOURCES SECURITY

8.1 PRIOR TO EMPLOYMENT
8.1.1 Roles and responsibilities
8.1.2 Screening
8.1.3 Terms and conditions of employment

8.2 DURING EMPLOYMENT
8.2.1 Management responsibilities
8.2.2 Information security awareness, education, and training
8.2.3 Disciplinary process

8.3 TERMINATION OR CHANGE OF EMPLOYMENT
8.3.1 Termination responsibilities
8.3.2 Return of assets
8.3.3 Removal of access rights

9 PHYSICAL AND ENVIRONMENTAL SECURITY

9.1 SECURE AREAS
9.1.1 Physical security perimeter
9.1.2 Physical entry controls
9.1.3 Securing offices, rooms, and facilities
9.1.4 Protecting against external and environmental threats
9.1.5 Working in secure areas
9.1.6 Public access, delivery, and loading areas

9.2 EQUIPMENT SECURITY
9.2.1 Equipment siting and protection
9.2.2 Supporting utilities
9.2.3 Cabling security

9.2.4 Equipment maintenance
9.2.5 Security of equipment off-premises
9.2.6 Secure disposal or re-use of equipment
9.2.7 Removal of property

10 COMMUNICATIONS AND OPERATIONS MANAGEMENT

10.1 OPERATIONAL PROCEDURES AND RESPONSIBILITIES
10.1.1 Documented operating procedures
10.1.2 Change management
10.1.3 Segregation of duties
10.1.4 Separation of development, test, and operational facilities

10.2 THIRD PARTY SERVICE DELIVERY MANAGEMENT
10.2.1 Service delivery
10.2.2 Monitoring and review of third party services
10.2.3 Managing changes to third party services

10.3 SYSTEM PLANNING AND ACCEPTANCE
10.3.1 Capacity management
10.3.2 System acceptance

10.4 PROTECTION AGAINST MALICIOUS AND MOBILE CODE
10.4.1 Controls against malicious code
10.4.2 Controls against mobile code

10.5 BACK-UP
10.5.1 Information back-up

10.6 NETWORK SECURITY MANAGEMENT
10.6.1 Network controls
10.6.2 Security of network services

10.7 MEDIA HANDLING
10.7.1 Management of removable media
10.7.2 Disposal of media
10.7.3 Information handling procedures
10.7.4 Security of system documentation

10.8 EXCHANGE OF INFORMATION
10.8.1 Information exchange policies and procedures
10.8.2 Exchange agreements
10.8.3 Physical media in transit
10.8.4 Electronic messaging
10.8.5 Business information systems

10.9 ELECTRONIC COMMERCE SERVICES
10.9.1 Electronic commerce
10.9.2 On-Line Transactions
10.9.3 Publicly available information

10.10 MONITORING
10.10.1 Audit logging
10.10.2 Monitoring system use
10.10.3 Protection of log information
10.10.4 Administrator and operator logs
10.10.5 Fault logging
10.10.6 Clock synchronization

11 ACCESS CONTROL

11.1 BUSINESS REQUIREMENT FOR ACCESS CONTROL
11.1.1 Access control policy

11.2 USER ACCESS MANAGEMENT
11.2.1 User registration
11.2.2 Privilege management
11.2.3 User password management
11.2.4 Review of user access rights

11.3 USER RESPONSIBILITIES
11.3.1 Password use
11.3.2 Unattended user equipment
11.3.3 Clear desk and clear screen policy

11.4 NETWORK ACCESS CONTROL
11.4.1 Policy on use of network services
11.4.2 User authentication for external connections
11.4.3 Equipment identification in networks
11.4.4 Remote diagnostic and configuration port protection
11.4.5 Segregation in networks
11.4.6 Network connection control
11.4.7 Network routing control

11.5 OPERATING SYSTEM ACCESS CONTROL
11.5.1 Secure log-on procedures
11.5.2 User identification and authentication
11.5.3 Password management system
11.5.4 Use of system utilities
11.5.5 Session time-out
11.5.6 Limitation of connection time

11.6 APPLICATION AND INFORMATION ACCESS CONTROL
11.6.1 Information access restriction
11.6.2 Sensitive system isolation

11.7 MOBILE COMPUTING AND TELEWORKING
11.7.1 Mobile computing and communications
11.7.2 Teleworking

12 INFORMATION SYSTEMS ACQUISITION, DEVELOPMENT AND MAINTENANCE

12.1 SECURITY REQUIREMENTS OF INFORMATION SYSTEMS
12.1.1 Security requirements analysis and specification

12.2 CORRECT PROCESSING IN APPLICATIONS
12.2.1 Input data validation
12.2.2 Control of internal processing
12.2.3 Message integrity
12.2.4 Output data validation

12.3 CRYPTOGRAPHIC CONTROLS
12.3.1 Policy on the use of cryptographic controls
12.3.2 Key management

12.4 SECURITY OF SYSTEM FILES
12.4.1 Control of operational software
12.4.2 Protection of system test data
12.4.3 Access control to program source code

12.5 SECURITY IN DEVELOPMENT AND SUPPORT PROCESSES
12.5.1 Change control procedures
12.5.2 Technical review of applications after operating system changes
12.5.3 Restrictions on changes to software packages
12.5.4 Information leakage
12.5.5 Outsourced software development

12.6 TECHNICAL VULNERABILITY MANAGEMENT
12.6.1 Control of technical vulnerabilities

13 INFORMATION SECURITY INCIDENT MANAGEMENT

13.1 REPORTING INFORMATION SECURITY EVENTS AND WEAKNESSES
13.1.1 Reporting information security events
13.1.2 Reporting security weaknesses

13.2 MANAGEMENT OF INFORMATION SECURITY INCIDENTS AND IMPROVEMENTS

13.2.1 Responsibilities and procedures

13.2.2 Learning from information security incidents

13.2.3 Collection of evidence

14 BUSINESS CONTINUITY MANAGEMENT

14.1 INFORMATION SECURITY ASPECTS OF BUSINESS CONTINUITY MANAGEMENT

14.1.1 Including information security in the business continuity manage ment process

14.1.2 Business continuity and risk assessment

14.1.3 Developing and implementing continuity plans including informa tion security

14.1.4 Business continuity planning framework

14.1.5 Testing, maintaining and re-assessing business continuity plans

15 COMPLIANCE

15.1 COMPLIANCE WITH LEGAL REQUIREMENTS

15.1.1 Identification of applicable legislation

15.1.2 Intellectual property rights (IPR)

15.1.3 Protection of organizational records

15.1.4 Data protection and privacy of personal information

15.1.5 Prevention of misuse of information processing facilities

15.1.6 Regulation of cryptographic controls

15.2 COMPLIANCE WITH SECURITY POLICIES AND STANDARDS, AND TECHNICAL COMPLIANCE

15.2.1 Compliance with security policies and standards

15.2.2 Technical compliance checking

15.3 INFORMATION SYSTEMS AUDIT CONSIDERATIONS

15.3.1 Information systems audit controls

15.3.2 Protection of information systems audit tools

Before investigating some clauses in more detail, some terminology mapping must be done.

Looking at Clause 8 above:

8 HUMAN RESOURCES SECURITY

8.1 PRIOR TO EMPLOYMENT

8.1.1 Roles and responsibilities

8.1.2 Screening

8.1.3 Terms and conditions of employment

8.2 DURING EMPLOYMENT

8.2.1 Management responsibilities
8.2.2 Information security awareness, education, and training
8.2.3 Disciplinary process

8.3 TERMINATION OR CHANGE OF EMPLOYMENT

8.3.1 Termination responsibilities
8.3.2 Return of assets
8.3.3 Removal of access rights

Clause 8 of ISO 27002 consists of three main security categories, 8.1, 8.2 and 8.3.

The main security category (8.1) has its own objective (not shown above), and three controls (8.1.1, 8.1.2 and 8.1.3) which can (should) be used to achieve the objective of 8.1.

ISO 27002 (page 23) contains five implementation guidances (not shown above), which can be used to implement the control 8.1.1.

This type of detail makes ISO 27002 an invaluable help for any ISM.

A little more detail is required here.

5.14.2 Some Sub-Clauses in More Detail

In this paragraph, more detailed view of one of the high-level clauses mentioned above is presented.

This will provide some more insight into the depth that ISO 27002 goes in providing guidance. Clause 11, which is on **Access Control**, is examined. By looking at the index above, it can be seen that there are seven main security categories in clause 11. They are 11.1–11.7. Main security category 11.3 will now be investigated a little deeper.

Again from the index above, it is clear that category 11.3 has three controls: 11.3.1–11.3.3. The content of 11.3.1 is:

"11.3.1 Password use

Control
Users should be required to follow good security practices in the selection and use of passwords.

Implementation guidance
All users should be advised to:

> *a) keep passwords confidential;*
> *b) avoid keeping a record (e.g. paper, software file or hand-held device) of passwords, unless this can be stored securely and the method of storing has been approved;*
> *c) change passwords whenever there is any indication of possible system or password compromise;*

d) select quality passwords with sufficient minimum length which are:

    1) easy to remember;

    2) not based on anything somebody else could easily guess or obtain using person related information, e.g., names, telephone numbers, and dates of birth etc.;

    3) not vulnerable to dictionary attacks (i.e., do not consist of words included in dictionaries);

    4) free of consecutive identical, all-numeric or all-alphabetic characters;

e) change passwords at regular intervals or based on the number of accesses (passwords for privileged accounts should be changed more frequently than normal passwords), and avoid re-using or cycling old passwords;

f) change temporary passwords at the first log-on;

g) not include passwords in any automated log-on process, e.g., stored in a macro or function key;

h) not share individual user passwords;

i) not use the same password for business and non-business purposes.

If users need to access multiple services, systems or platforms, and are required to maintain multiple separate passwords, they should be advised that they may use a single, quality password (see d) above) for all services where the user is assured that a reasonable level of protection has been established for the storage of the password within each service, system or platform.

Other information

*   Management of the help desk system dealing with lost or forgotten passwords needs special care as this may also be a means of attack to the password system."*

Therefore, to implement proper (logical) Access Control according to ISO 27002, one of the controls which should be enforced, is proper password use (11.3.1). In order to enforce such proper password use, the implementation guidances which should be used are those listed as a) to i) above.

It should be clear from the detailed guidance given for password use, how valuable this document can be in the process of Information Security Governance.

As stated several times, ISO 27002 is a guideline, and is in no way compulsory. However, companies can commit to this guideline in such a way that they create a formal Information Security Management System (ISMS) which they then get formally certificated as conforming to the provisions of ISO 27001.

This process is discussed in the next paragraph.

5.15 The Certification Process Against ISO 27001

Once the company has established such an Information Security Management System (ISMS), and conforms to all the requirements as set out in the ISO 27001 Standard, the company can request a suitably qualified ISO 27001 Auditor to formally audit the ISMS against the set standard. If the ISMS conforms to the requirements of the standard, the company can receive a formal certificate that its ISMS complies with the Standard ISO 27001.

ISO 27002 is, of course, closely linked to ISO 27001, and the requirements to which the ISMS must conform, are precisely those specified in ISO 27001.

However, it must be understood that:

- ISO 27002 is a guideline, that is, nothing in the document is compulsory. A company can decide to use parts of or all the document, or implement some clauses partially or merely use it as a good reference document. Conformance or non-conformance is up to the company.
- ISO 27001, on the other hand, is a standard, and to eventually get certified, a company MUST conform to everything specified in the document. If the company decide to not conform, or not implement any clause or sub-clause, the decision must be properly motivated, based on some form of risk analysis which supports the decision.

ISO 27001 exactly and precisely specifies how the ISMS must be created and operated.

The following comes directly from ISO 27001:

This International Standard (ISO 27001) has been prepared to provide a model for establishing, implementing, operating, monitoring, reviewing, maintaining and improving an Information Security Management System (ISMS).

It is expected that an ISMS implementation will be scaled in accordance with the needs of the organization, e.g. a simple situation requires a simple ISMS solution.

This International Standard can be used in order to assess conformance by interested internal and external parties.

The following aspects are required by ISO 27001 as far as the ISMS is concerned. These aspects are merely listed to give an idea of what is required

5.15.1 General Requirements of the ISMS:

The organization shall develop, implement, maintain and continually improve a documented ISMS within the context of the organization's overall business activities and risk.

5.15.2 *Establishing and Managing the ISMS*

The cycle, represented by the four steps below, is at the core of establishing, implementing, monitoring, reviewing, maintaining and improving the ISMS:

Plan (establish the ISMS)	Establish ISMS policy, objectives, processes and procedures relevant to managing risk and improving information security to deliver results in accordance with an organization's overall policies and objectives.
Do (implement and operate the ISMS)	Implement and operate the ISMS policy, controls, processes and procedures.
Check (monitor and review the ISMS)	Assess and, where applicable, measure process performance against ISMS policy, objectives and practical experience and report the results to management for review.
Act (maintain and improve the ISMS)	Take corrective and preventive actions, based on the results of the internal ISMS audit and management review or other relevant information, to achieve continual improvement of the ISMS.

(www.iso.ch)

The standard also demands specific strict documentation requirements for the ISMS, Management responsibility towards the ISMS, Management review of the ISMS and continual improvement of the ISMS.

A list of companies which have created such an ISMS, and which have had it formally certified against ISO 27001, can be found at http://www.17799central.com/cert.htm (as of January 2008).

5.16 Summary

This chapter has introduced two best practice frameworks for Information Security Governance. From the Information Security Governance/Management viewpoint, COBIT and ISO 27002 provide excellent frameworks within which Information Security Governance/Management can be placed, forming an integral part of Information Technology Governance.

In each of the next 5 chapters, one further component of the Model, as introduced in Fig. 4.2, will be discussed.

References

1. ISO/IEC 27002 (2005). Information Technology–Security Techniques–Code of Practice for Information Security Management. International Organization for Standardization. Available from www.iso.ch
2. Von Solms, SH (2005) Information Security Governance: COBIT or ISO 17799 or Both? Computers & Security, 24(2), 99–104

Chapter 6
The Direct Part of the Model – An Information Security Policy Architecture

6.1 Introduction

In Chapter 4, the Model for Information Security Governance was introduced. One of the main characteristics of the Model is the Direct/Control Cycle, which represents the fact that top-down directing takes place over all levels of management, and bottom-up control takes place, again over all levels. The two actions of Direct and Control ensure that proper governance is enforced throughout the whole cycle.

This chapter discusses the Direct part of the cycle in detail and it will be shown how Directives from the Strategic Level are expanded, on the Tactical Level, to a Corporate Information Security Policy, and how that is again expanded into detailed policies, procedures and standards. Each of these sub-policies is then again expanded on the Operational Level to administrative and operational procedures.

This chapter will, therefore, be dedicated to Information Security Governance-related directives, policies, detailed sub-policies and procedures. All the documents will be organized in an Information Security Policy Architecture (ISPA) which is actually the output of the whole Direct Cycle.

Before doing that, firstly what some international best practices say about Information Security policies, procedures, etc, will be discussed

6.2 ISO 27002 on Policy Aspects

Clause 5 of ISO 27002 [1] requires Management to issue and ensure the maintenance of an Information Security Policy (document) across the organization.

In Paragraph 0.6 of ISO 27002, an Information Security Policy document is seen as common practice and, therefore, an essential component of any Information Security plan.

Control 5.5.1 states very clearly that an Information Security Policy document:

- must exist;
- must have been approved by senior management; and
- all parties mentioned in the scope of the Policy must be aware of the policy and its content.

S.H. von Solms, R. von Solms, *Information Security Governance*,
DOI 10.1007/978-0-387-79984-1_6, © Springer Science+Business Media, LLC 2009

Clause 5 is very important to anyone who wants to draft an Information Security Policy as it provides guidance on aspects like:

- the type of statements that should be included in such an Information Security Policy;
- the way in which the Policy should be communicated and reviewed;

6.3 COBIT on Policy Aspects

Control Objective DS 5.2 concerns itself with an IT Security Plan, and requires the drafting and implementation of Information Security Policies and Procedures.

The next paragraphs concentrate on these required policy components of the Model, specifically as far as the type of documents required by the Direct Cycle and their mutual relationship is concerned [2].

6.4 Information Security Governance-Related Documents Produced in the Direct Part of the Direct/Control Cycle

6.4.1 The Documents

The Information Security-related documents which will be considered in the rest of this chapter include:

- A Board-initiated Directive concerning Information Security Governance;
- A Corporate Information Security Policy flowing from the Directive;
- A set of detailed sub-policies flowing from the Corporate Information Security Policy;
- A set of company standards based on the Corporate and Detailed Policies;
- A set of administrative and operational procedures, again flowing from the detailed set of sub-policies.

Remember that in Chapter 4, the concept of 'measurability' was introduced. It stated that "*it is essential to ensure that all documents produced during the top-down 'direct' part of the cycle, must in principle, be formulated in such a way that the contents can be measured in some way.*"

All of the documents mentioned above, and contained in the ISPA introduced in figure 6.1 below, will therefore contain a **Compliance Clause** specifying in which way compliance to the specific document will be measured. In this chapter, these Compliance Clauses will be left empty. Chapter 7, which covers the Control part of the cycle, will come back to these clauses as far as content is concerned. In the meantime, in this chapter they are merely place holders.

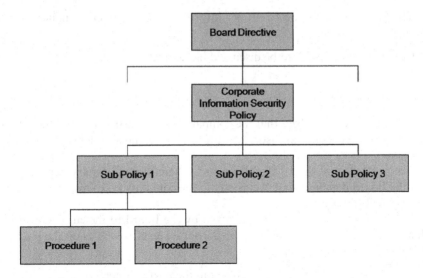

Fig. 6.1 The information security policy architecture

6.4.2 The Structure

All these documents together form an ISPA, as illustrated below.

Note that the Board Directive need not necessarily be totally dedicated to Information Security aspects, but must contain enough content to drive and motivate the creation and existence of the Corporate Information Security Policy (CISP).

6.4.3 The Board Directive

This Board Directive can come in many forms, and some examples are given below. The important aspect, however, is that the Directive must indicate the realization by the Board of the importance of the company's IT assets to the company, and contain the mandate from the Board to protect these assets.

6.4.3.1 Example 1

The Board of XXX accepts the importance of the company's IT infrastructure in furthering the strategic goals of the company. The Board also realizes the potential impact it can have on the company, and the consequences to the company if this IT infrastructure is compromised in any way.

For this reason, the Board demands a proper environment to protect the IT infrastructure against any disruptions or compromises.

The Board fully supports a proper Information Security Governance environment for XXX.

Compliance Clause: <to be discussed in the next chapter>

6.4.3.2 Example 2

The Board of XXX realizes that the company's IT infrastructure and the information processed by this infrastructure are among the most valuable assets of the company.

The protection of these valuable assets is, therefore, of primary importance, and the Board demands that everybody in the company takes responsibility to help protect these assets.

Full support and commitment is given by the Board to the enforcement of all aspects of Information Security on corporate level as well as on the level of every individual employee.

Compliance Clause: <to be discussed in the next chapter>

With such a type of Board Directive as input or driver, a Corporate Information Security Policy must now be created. This is discussed in the next paragraph.

6.4.4 The Corporate Information Security Policy (CISP)

The CISP flows directly from the Board's Directive, and is a high-level document providing a basis for all lower-level documents related to Information Security. Let us first investigate some requirements or specifications for the CISP.

Although such policies come in different forms, the following are guidelines which, if followed, will help to create a proper CISP and, therefore, a comprehensive ISPA:

- The CISP must indicate Board and executive management support and commitment and it must be clear that the CISP flows from a higher-level directive;
- The CISP must be accepted and signed by the CEO or equivalent officer;
- The CISP must not be a long document, nor must it be written in a technical form. The maximum length should be about four to five pages, and it must contain high-level statements concerning Information Security;
- The CISP should not change very often, and must be 'stable' as far as technical developments and changes are concerned;
- For the reason mentioned above, the CISP must not contain any references to specific technologies, and must be 'technology neutral';
- The CISP must indicate who is the owner of the Policy, and what the responsibilities of other relevant people are
- The CISP must clearly indicate the Scope of the Policy, that is, all people who will be subject to the Policy;

- The CISP must refer to possible (disciplinary) actions for non-conformance to the CISP and its lower-level constituent policies;
- The CISP must be distributed as widely as possible in the company, and must be covered in all relevant awareness courses;
- The CISP must have a **Compliance Clause.**

The following sample CISP contains most of the aspects mentioned above.

6.4.4.1 Example

The XXX Corporate Information Security Policy

Final Version: (date)
Review Date: (date)
Author: <Name 1>
Owner: <Name 2>

Contents

1. The importance of information to XXX

2. What is Information Security?

3. Why XXX needs Information Security

4. The Information Security Commitment of XXX's Board

5. Scope

6. Information Security Statements in this Corporate Information Security Policy

7. Responsibilities

8. Compliance Clause <to be discussed in the next chapter>

1. The importance of information to XXX

XXX is a company which is IT intensive, meaning that most, if not all of XXX's operations are highly integrated and dependant on its IT assets. These IT assets include the data and information of customers, employees, etc, as well as the information processing systems which store, process and transmit these assets.

Therefore, these IT assets, in all their forms, can be seen as the life blood of XXX, and must, therefore, be suitably protected against all risks. Properly protecting and securing these IT assets are critical to XXX's survival.

Furthermore, XXX is subject to a wide range of legislative, regulatory and contractual agreements and specifications, which also require the proper protection and security of all these IT assets.

The purpose of this Corporate Information Security Policy is to state the commitment and support of management to such protection and security, and to specify the environment which will be used in XXX to protect these IT assets from all types of threats, whether internal or external, deliberate or accidental.

2. What is Information Security?

Information Security is seen as the discipline used to maintain the following three basic characteristics of information and data:

Confidentiality, Integrity and Availability

This Policy therefore specifies the environment which will exist in XXX to ensure that the confidentiality, integrity and availability of XXX's IT assets and information processing systems are maintained at all times.

3. Why XXX needs Information Security

As stated above, XXX's IT assets are critical to XXX's survival.

However, for XXX to be a competitive player in the market, XXX must also share such information assets with other external players, for example, customers, financial institutions, etc. This sharing, of course, results in increased risks to these vital XXX information assets.

To protect XXX's information assets during internal as well as external use, and also to conform to legislative, contractual and statutory requirements regarding its IT assets, Information Security is one of XXX's prime responsibilities in order to protect and secure these vital assets.

This responsibility is shared by all employees of XXX – from the highest to the lowest level.

4. The Information Security Commitment of XXX's Board

The Board of XXX realizes the strategic importance of its IT assets and information processing systems, and the subsequent protection of these assets.

Full support and commitment is given by the Board to the enforcement of all aspects of Information Security on all levels of XXX.

This commitment is formulated in terms of the following Policy statements, and the Board also mandates disciplinary action against any stakeholder of XXX who does not comply with the content of this Corporate Information Security Policy and its constituent sub-policies.

5. Scope

This Policy applies to:

5.1 All XXX's IT assets stored, processed and distributed via XXX's information processing systems;

5.2 Any person who had been granted authorization to access XXX's IT resources, including, but not limited to, permanent, temporary, third party, contractual employees and users;

5.3 All business partners and clients that access XXX's IT assets in any way.

6. Information Security Statements in this Corporate Information Security Policy
Statement 6.1

XXX will have a proper Information Security organizational structure to manage Information Security according to this Corporate Information Security Policy and its constituent sub-policies.
This structure will:

- ensure that security roles be assigned to all users;
- that all users are aware of the content of this Policy;
- that all users are aware of the disciplinary consequences of not complying with this Policy;
- coordinate and review the continuous implementation of this Policy.

Statement 6.2

All IT assets in XXX will have a documented way in which they are handled, including:

- being reflected in a company-wide inventory;
- having a nominated owner who will ensure proper rules for the handling and protection of such assets.

Statement 6.3

XXX's Personnel (Human Resource) policies must incorporate detailed measures to support the implementation of this Corporate Information Security Policy. These measures must include termination of employment, non-disclosure and confidentiality clauses, job-oriented

Information Security responsibilities and reference to disciplinary action for non-conformance.

Statement 6.4
XXX will have a proper infrastructure to enforce physical and environmental security in order to protect information-related assets.

Statement 6.5
XXX will have the proper measures, including responsibilities and procedures, in place to ensure the correct and proper management and operation of all its information processing and communications facilities.

Statement 6.6
XXX will have the proper measures in place to ensure that only properly authorized people have (logical) access to its information facilities.

Statement 6.7
XXX will have proper measures in place to ensure that Information Security is taken into account during the acquisition, development and maintenance of all software systems.

Statement 6.8
XXX will have a proper system for managing Information Security incidents.

Statement 6.9
XXX will have proper measures in place to ensure the business continuity of all its information processing systems.

Statement 6.10
XXX will have proper measures in place to ensure compliance to all legal requirements, as well as to the Statements of this Corporate Information Security Policy.

This XXX Corporate Information Technology Security Policy is supported by the set of XXX's Information Security Sub-Policies in which each of the Statements above is specified in detail.

7. **Responsibilities**

   7.1 Senior Management
   7.2 Information Security Manager
   7.3 Business Systems' Owners
   7.4 Risk Management/Audit Department
   7.5 User

   Note that this Responsibility list is not comprehensive, but merely acts as an example.

8. **Compliance Clause** <to be discussed in the nest chapter>

Fig. 6.3 Example of an acceptable internet use information security policy

By closely comparing the Clauses in ISO 27002 and the Statements in the Policy above, the reader should see a clear correspondence.

6.4.5 The Information Security Sub-Policies

As indicated in Fig. 6.2 above, and as contained in XXX's example above, the CISP is supported by a set of Information Security Sub-Policies, also known as secondary policies or lower-level policies.

This set of Sub-Policies may differ from company to company, but usually the following ones will be apparent:

- A Malicious Software Control Policy (Anti-Virus Policy)
- An Acceptable Internet Usage Policy
- An Acceptable Email Usage Policy
- A Logical Access Control Policy
- A Disaster Recovery (Backup) Policy
- A Remote Access Control Policy
- A Third Party Access Control Policy.

These Sub-Policies define specific important aspects in more detail. It is very important that the ISPA clearly indicate where these different policies originate – this means that any policy on this level must be able to be 'linked' or 'traced back' to the CISP in some way. The ISPA is, therefore, a hierarchical structure which links everything to everything. No Sub-Policies should 'hang loose' without indicating why it is there and where it originated from.

Each of these Sub-Policies must have a **Compliance Clause.**

In the case of the CISP above, a possible list of Sub-Policies referred to after Statement 6.10 is provided below.

The following are XXX Sub-Policies for Information Security flowing from XXX's CISP:

1. XXX Internet Acceptable Usage Policy
2. XXX eMail Acceptable Use Policy
3. Malicious Software Protection Policy
4. Back-up Policy
5. E-Mail Policy
6. Internet Usage Policy
7. Information Security Incident Policy
8. Network Security Policy
9. Logical Access Policy
10. Physical and Environmental Security Policy
11. Third Party Access Policy
12. Remote Access Policy
13. Information Security Awareness Policy
14. Data Classification Policy
15. End User Computing Policy.

Each of these Sub-Policies is again supported by a set of Information Security Procedures specifying how specific things must be done (See Fig. 6.1).

As an example, the XXX Internet Acceptable Usage Policy (number 1 in the list above) may look as follows:

6.4.5.1 Example

The XXX Internet Acceptable Use Information Security Policy

Final Version: (date)
Review Date: (date)
Author: <name 1>

1. **Introduction**

XXX currently supplies an Internet access service that is available to all authorized XXX and employees. This access empowers Internet users to access information and exchange information with colleagues and peers around the world, as well as with suppliers and customers. It also allows employees to download research data, scientific papers, policies, directives and other information which saves both time and money over requesting these information and documents to be faxed or mailed.

With this empowerment also comes responsibility. Many employees rely on this Internet Service to successfully do their work.

Misuse of the Internet Service will negatively impact on the quality of the service as well as the cost of providing the service, and employees that cannot function without the service may be impacted negatively.

Some restrictions on the use of the Internet Service are necessary to ensure that the service will be available when needed by XXX employees for work-related tasks.

To aid employees in their use of the Internet Service, this Acceptable Use Policy document was drafted. The XXX Internet Service is not to be used for private gain or profit.

World-wide incidents of misuse and abuse of networks connected to the Internet by hackers or overly curious network users have necessitated certain limitations to be imposed in order to ensure the continued security and integrity of the network. As long as activity is related to and necessary for the completion of a person's work, then that activity is generally considered an authorized use of the Internet Service and is allowed.

2. **Scope**

The scope of this Sub-Policy is the same as the scope of XXX's Corporate Information Security Policy.

3. **Reference**
   3.1 Up
   Statements 6.5 and 6.6 in XXX's Corporate Information Security Policy give origin to this Sub-Policy.
   3.2 Down
   The following lower level procedure supports this Sub-Policy.
   'Application Procedure for XXX Internet Service Connectivity'

4. **Owner <name>**
5. **Main Policy Statement**

Use of the XXX Internet Service must be in support of official XXX work or activities.
   Sub-Statements supporting the main Statement

   Statement 5.1
   Use of the XXX Internet Service must be in support of official XXX work or activities. All user requests for XXX Internet Service connectivity must be approved and supported by the employee's line Manager. Requests for Internet Service must be done using the specified procedure 'Application Procedure for XXX Internet Service Connectivity'.

   Statement 5.2
   It will be the responsibility of the user's line Manager to ensure that the user does not misuse the Internet Service.

   Statement 5.3
   Only individual IDs will be allowed. No group or shared IDs will be allocated.

Statement 5.4

The user who applied for the access will be held responsible and accountable for the ID and all actions taken with the ID. This means that it is up to the user to keep his password secret, and change it at regular intervals or when it leaked out to other users.

Statement 5.5

Any misuse of the ID will lead to suspension of access to the Internet. Misuse of an ID include actions like excessive use not related to XXX activities, accessing of offensive sites, downloading offensive material or games, failure to follow licensing requirements on software downloaded from the Internet, failure to scan downloaded software for viruses, unnecessary file downloads during working hours and hacking activities.

Access to certain sites will be blocked by the firewall. This will include sites that may be offensive to users, games sites, etc.

Statement 5.6

Since the XXX Internet Service and resources are provided to support the work of XXX, there is no personal expectation of privacy. Information flowing to and from the Internet may be logged and may be reviewed by Managers, Supervisors, Internal Audit and other authorized individuals at any time. Additionally, Internet activity is recorded and periodically examined for security and policy compliance purposes.

Statement 5.7

Like other forms of misconduct, misuse of XXX Internet resources is grounds for disciplinary action.

Statement 5.8

Use of the XXX Internet Service for personal training and further education is acceptable if it is XXX work related.

Statement 5.9

The XXX Internet Service may not be used for the introduction of worms, viruses, Trojans, or other software that maliciously interfere with normal XXX Internet service operations or the operation of any other outside network. Such acts may be, in some cases, criminal offences if a user's action interferes with the operation of outside networks that are not part of XXX.

The use of the XXX Internet Service is inappropriate when that use:

- Compromises the privacy of users and their personal data;
- Damages the integrity of a computer system, or the data or programs stored on a computer system;
- Disrupts the intended use of system or network resources;
- Misuse resources (time, network bandwidth);
- Uses or copies proprietary software when not authorized to do so;
- Uses a computer system as a conduit for unauthorized access attempts on other computer systems (hacking).

6. **Responsibilities**

   6.1 Line Managers
   6.2 User
   6.3 Policy Owner(s)

7. **Compliance Clause** <to be discussed in the next chapter>

Fig. 6.3 Example of an acceptable internet use information security policy

6.4.6 The Procedures

Every Sub-Policy has, as indicated in Fig. 6.3, a set of Procedures which specify how its aspects must be implemented.

Consider the **XXX Internet Acceptable Use Information Security Policy** presented above.

Statement 5.1 states:

> Use of the XXX Internet Service must be in support of official XXX work or activities. All user requests for XXX Internet service connectivity must be approved and supported by the employee's line Manager. Requests for Internet Service must be done using the specified procedure: 'Application Procedure for XXX Internet Service Connectivity'.

Although this Sub-Policy has only one supporting Procedure, some other Sub-Policies may have several such procedures supporting a specific Sub-Policy.

Again, each of these Procedures must have a Compliance Clause included.

6.4.6.1 Example

The XXX Application Procedure for Internet Service Connectivity

  Final Version: (date)
  Review Date: (date)
  Author: <Name 1>
  Owner: < Name 2>

This Procedure follows from Statement 5.1 in XXX's Internet Acceptable Use Information Security Policy.

1. Surname :
2. Initials :
3. Department :
4. Office number :
5. Telephone extension :
6. Home phone number :

  I have read XXX's Corporate Information Security Policy, as well as the XXX Internet Acceptable Use Information Security Policy. I understand the content, and if access is granted to me, I will use it in line with these stated Policies.

Signature of Applicant :   Date :

  I am satisfied that the applicant needs the access applied for, and that the applicant is aware of the policies governing the specific access

Line Manager's Signature :   Date :

Information Security Officer's Signature :   Date :

Compliance Clause : <to be discussed in the next chapter>

6.5 Summary

This chapter looked at the 'Direct' part of the Model for Information Security Governance. This mainly concentrated on the aspect of policies, procedures and standards. The idea of a hierarchical Information Security Policy Architecture (ISPA) was introduced, and four levels of this architecture were investigated.

This began by looking at the Board Directive on the highest (first) level, then looking at the Corporate Information Security Policy at the second level, one Sub-Policy at the third level and one Procedure at the fourth level.

Creating all the components of this ISPA for a company is a big project, but basically it goes along the lines as discussed in this chapter.

The next chapter investigates the 'Control' part of the Model.

References

1. ISO/IEC 27002 (2005). Information Technology – Security Techniques – Code of Practice for Information Security Management. International Organization for Standardization. Available from www.iso.ch
2. COBIT (2005). Control Objectives for Information and Related Technology. Available from ISACA www.isaca.org

Chapter 7
The Control Part of the Model – An Information Security Compliance Management Environment

7.1 Introduction

The Model for Information Security Governance, introduced in Chapter 4, clearly indicated that there is a compliance component which is essential. This compliance component is basically to ensure that all the elements of the Direct component are being complied with, and that, therefore, all IT risks are managed in an acceptable way. Chapter 6 introduced the Direct component, and this chapter investigates how the compliance component can be enforced.

Before doing that, what some international best practices say about this type of compliance enforcement must first be investigated. After that, ways will be discussed in which this compliance component can be implemented.

7.2 ISO 27002 on Compliance Aspects

Clause 15 of ISO 27002 [1] is totally dedicated to compliance, and has the following controls related to it:

7.2.1   Compliance with legal requirements (control 15.1)
7.2.2   Compliance with Security Policies and standards, and technical compliance (control 15.2)
7.2.3   Information systems audit compliance (control 15.3).

This chapter will specifically concentrate on 7.2.2 above, this sub-clause states:

Objective: to ensure compliance with organizational policies and standards.

It is, therefore, clear that enforcing and ensuring compliance with policies, procedures and standards is advised by this leading international Best Practice.

S.H. von Solms, R. von Solms, *Information Security Governance*,
DOI 10.1007/978-0-387-79984-1_7, © Springer Science+Business Media, LLC 2009

7.3 COBIT on Compliance Aspects

The high-level processes ME 1 to ME 4 are totally dedicated to Monitoring and Evaluating. Specifically, control ME 4.7 emphasizes the importance of the assurance of conformance to the organization's policies, standards and procedures [2].

Within DS 5 on Systems Security, control objective DS 5.5 provides guidance on Security Testing, Surveillance and Monitoring.

Therefore, this leading international Best Practice also places a great deal of emphasis on the aspect of compliance monitoring and enforcement.

7.4 Compliance Enforcement

ISO 27002 and COBIT are, therefore, clear on the aspect of monitoring and ensuring compliance as part of Information Security Governance (ISG). As stated, the rest of this chapter will concentrate on ensuring compliance with the documents which are part of the ISPA.

In Chapter 6, the Direct part of the Model was investigated. This part basically consisted of a set of documents providing direction as far as the protection of a company's IT assets is concerned.

This set of documents was called an Information Security Policy Architecture (ISPA).

As discussed in Chapter 4, the Control part of the model checks and ensures that the documents within the ISPA are actually being conformed to and, therefore, ensures compliance with these documents.

For that reason, every document, or every clause in a document from the ISPA must have some type of Compliance Clause to indicate in what way compliance to the specific document and/or clause will be evaluated. Provision for these clauses was made in the documents of the ISPA in Chapter 6. The purpose of this chapter is to give some guidelines on what these clauses can contain, that is, to provide some ideas on how compliance can be checked and then enforced.

There are no clear guidelines on how the Control part of the Model, that is, compliance checking and enforcement must be done. It is, and stays, a very difficult issue, but that it is important and must be done, lies at the heart of good ISG.

This chapter will not, therefore, give specific solutions to the problem, but will rather discuss the issue, and give some examples of how it can be done.

7.5 The Traditional Approach to Control and Compliance Monitoring

In most companies, some form of compliance management is done by the ICT Audit Section. This section performs, from time to time, some type of ICT audit, in which a range of controls are monitored and checked, and an Audit Report is created as output of this process. In general, such a report highlights

problems as far as the protection of the company's ICT assets are concerned –
sometimes even indicating that the company does not have an Information
Security Policy of any kind.

Such ICT audits are important, and do play an important part in the Control
part of the Model.

However, in modern times, where ICT is so strategic to and integrated into
the running of a company, it is no longer acceptable to have such an ICT audit
report once every year or even once every six months. To find out six months
after a person had left the company that his/her logon and access rights are still
active on the company's ICT systems creates unacceptable risks to the company. If such rights are still active a day after the person has left, they should be
picked up and reported in order to delete them.

Compliance enforcement must, therefore, have a much more immediate,
dynamic and even real-time character than it has in most cases today.

More than merely the traditional ICT Internal Audit is needed to have a
successful Control part of the model, i.e., to enforce proper compliance with the
relevant ISPA.

As already stated in Chapter 6, in order to really measure compliance to a specific
policy or procedure, that policy or procedure must contain a Compliance Clause,
specifying how compliance to this policy or procedure is to be determined and
enforced. If it is not possible, or extremely difficult to define any type of Compliance
Clause for a specific policy, then the content of the policy must be re-examined, and
simplified. It is really not of any value to have a policy which is formulated in such a
way that it is not possible to monitor compliance with that policy.

Suppose, for example, some Information Security Policy has a statement to
the effect that: **'Employees must take Information Security seriously'**. This is not
a good statement because ensuring compliance with this statement is very
difficult, if not impossible.

The rest of this chapter will now expand on this Compliance Clause, and give
some examples.

Paragraph 7.8 will then present an example of a dynamic Compliance
Management System.

7.6 The Compliance Management Clause

7.6.1 Compliance Clause for the Board Directive

Let us revisit the Board Directive on Information Security as introduced in
Paragraph 6.4.3.1. The Directives read as follows:

> The Board of XXX accepts the importance of the company's IT infrastructure in
> furthering the strategic goals of the company. The Board also realizes the potential
> impact it can have on the company, and the consequences to the company if this IT
> infrastructure is compromised in any way.

For this reason, the Board demands a proper environment to protect the IT infrastructure against any disruptions or compromises.

The Board fully supports a proper ISG environment for XXX.

Compliance Clause: <to be discussed in the next chapter>

In order to monitor and manage compliance with this Directive, the Compliance Clause must indicate what is required in order to be able to test or measure compliance to this specific Directive.

One possible formulation of the Compliance Clause above can be:

Compliance Clause:

The Board requires a proper feedback, every three months, of the level of compliance with this Directive.

This formulation is very wide, but at least it demands a feedback on a regular basis.

Another possible formulation of the Compliance Clause can be:

Compliance Clause:

The Board requires a detailed feedback, every three months, of any serious risks which may compromise the protection of XXX's ICT infrastructure.

Again, this Compliance Clause is very wide and does not specifically address every aspect in the Directive. To have a Compliance Clause addressing all aspects the Directive may be very difficult, but the challenge is to create a clause which will be able to measure compliance in the best possible way.

As can be seen above, there is no clearly defined way in which the Compliance Clause should be formulated – that is still quite difficult, but that such a clause should exist, and at least give some indication of how compliance with the relevant Directive or policy should be measured, is essential.

7.6.2 Compliance Clauses for the Corporate Information Security Policy

This Policy was introduced in Chapter 6, but with an empty Compliance Clause.

The challenge now is how to formulate the relevant Compliance Clause. It will be very difficult to define a sensible single Compliance Clause for the complete Policy, so we will have to break it up into a number of such clauses. One possibility is to have a Compliance Clause for each of the ten Statements in the Policy. Here are some examples of such an approach.

Statement 6.1

XXX will have a proper Information Security organizational structure to manage Information Security according to this CISP and its constituent sub-policies.

This structure will:

- *ensure that security roles be assigned to all users;*
- *that all users are aware of the content of this Policy;*

- *that all users are aware of the disciplinary consequences of not complying with this Policy;*
- *coordinate and review the continuous implementation of this Policy.*

A possible Compliance Clause for Statement 6.1:

The effectiveness of XXX's Information Security organizational structure in managing and enforcing the requirements of the company's ISPA shall be evaluated every six months and the results incorporated in higher-level reporting.

Another possible Compliance Clause for Statement 6.1:

The way the Information Security function in XXX is organized, and the reporting structures within this function shall be evaluated every 12 months to ensure that the structure stays adequate to ensure the proper protection of all the electronic assets of XXX. The results of this evaluation will be part of the annual evaluation and reporting of organizational structures in the company.

Again, note the fact that no exact and unique Compliance Clause exists. As long as the Clause defines some way in which the effectiveness of the relevant policy statement can be determined, it can be acceptable. Of course, the more refined it is, the better.

A few more examples are now investigated.

Statement 6.6

XXX will have the proper measures in place to ensure that only properly authorized people have (logical) access to its information facilities.

A possible Compliance Clause for Statement 6.6:

A daily report of all unauthorized logical access, or attempts to perform unauthorized logical access, will be produced. Any discrepancies will be acted on and escalated to higher authorities.

Note that this clause is a little more detailed, but it is not stated explicitly how such a report should be compiled – that detail does not appear on this level.

Let us look at Statement 6.9.

Statement 6.9

XXX will have proper measures in place to ensure the business continuity of all its information processing systems.

A possible Compliance Clause for Statement 6.9:

The business continuity system of XXX will be tested every six months, and the results of such tests will be incorporated in reporting to Executive Management.

7.7 Notes on the Idea of Compliance Clauses

From the examples above, the following comments about the idea of Compliance Clauses can be made:

- The cycle of compliance checking, specified by the relevant clause, can differ between clauses. For 6.1 it can be evaluated only every six months, while for Statement 6.6, it should be daily. Precisely what these cycles are is determined by the company, depending on their specific risk situation.
- It is also very important to realize that if, for example, it is not possible to compile the report required for Statement 6.6, that is, the necessary infrastructure is not available in the company, then it is actually a waste of time to have Statement 6.6 in the Policy at all because then it is not possible to manage Statement 6.6. Remember, you can only manage what you can measure!
- Every Compliance Clause will, in many cases, be supported by more detailed specifications on precisely how the information needed to conform to the Clause must be acquired, how it must be consolidated, etc. The Compliance Management System, discussed in Paragraph 7.8, as well as the idea of Service Level Agreements, introduced in Chapter 9, will make these aspects clearer.

As stated several times, there is no specific way in which the Compliance Clauses must be formulated, and what the cycle of monitoring should be. This is an area where a lot of research still needs to be done, but the importance of this approach to properly enforce ISG cannot be over emphasized.

The big challenge is to formulate such clauses, and then to create ways and means to be able to acquire the required information needed by the specific Compliance Clause. If the Compliance Clause for Statement 6.6 is again looked at, there need to be ways and means to acquire a lot of information on a daily basis to determine if any unauthorized attempts have taken place.

Furthermore, this data and information must be aggregated so as to create higher-level reports. Executive Management cannot be flooded with pages of detailed reports: all the acquired information must try to be summarized in such a way that it can be presented in an easily understandable way to Executive Management.

The following paragraphs discuss prototype system which was developed and to prove the concept of compliance management.

7.8 An Example of an Information Security Compliance Management System[1]

7.8.1 Introduction

This paragraph expands on the idea of Information Security Compliance Management by discussing an example of an operational Information Security Compliance Management system and methodology. It must be noted that the example discussed in this paragraph does not precisely fit the discussion above,

---

[1] This is a prototype proof of concept system, and was developed based on an open software approach. All development was done by Francois Meyer.

that is, using Compliance Clauses in Policy documents. It was developed from another angle, and is included here to show that it is possible to monitor and measure and then manage – that is, to enforce compliance through monitoring and measurement.

Compliance Management enforcement (as related to ISG) is seen as all those compliance enforcement mechanisms needed to ensure that compliance to all Information Security policies and procedures are enforced, and to ensure that IT risks are properly mediated and managed.

For good ISG, good ITG and good Corporate Governance, Information Security Compliance Management and Information Security Operational Management should be seen as different dimensions of ISG, and should be housed and treated differently. This aspect is discussed in more detail in Chapter 9.

In this paragraph we will discuss an example of a **Compliance Management Approach** (CMA) which was developed to measure and monitor compliance to IT risks in a company, and to report the status of these to Executive Management in an easily understandable way. The CMA consists of two components:

- an underlying database system and
- a methodology.

For such a system to operate properly, the following aspects are essential, and must be addressed:

- Which IT risks do we want to monitor?
- What data do we need to monitor the status of these risks?
- In what way do we report the results to Executive Management so that they can understand the situation?

First the database of the system will be discussed, and then the way the methodology operates. This discussion will also address the three aspects mentioned above.

7.8.2 The System

7.8.2.1 Determining the IT Risks to be Monitored

As mentioned above, there needs to be a good understanding of the IT risks to monitor and manage. It is also essential that these risks be identified as business risks by the business people (system owners) and not as technical risks by the technical people.

In this approach, COBIT (see Chapters 2 and 5) was used as the basis for identifying the IT risks which need to be managed. The fact that COBIT is today accepted as an international Best Practice for ITG makes it a logical choice as a reference framework. This system is based on COBIT 3 and, therefore, the structure differs a little from that discussed in Chapter 5.

From the 318 Detailed Control Objectives (DCOs) of COBIT 3, 62 were selected as having a direct impact on Information Security Management. These 62 DCOs included the 21 from DS 5, the section of COBIT directly related to Information Security. The rest (41) were selected as a result of their (indirect) importance and relevance to Information Security Management. (What COBIT 3 calls Detailed Control Objectives are called COs in COBIT 4.1).

Each of these selected 62 DCOs was then seen as giving rise to an IT risk if the specific DCO was not be properly managed.

The system, therefore, defined 62 different IT risks, based on the 62 DCOs selected from COBIT. These 62 DCOs were stored in a data base.

The next step was to ascertain what information or data were needed to determine if the specific DCO, or IT risk, was properly managed. For this COBIT's set of Control Practices (CPs) was used.

7.8.2.2 Determining the Data needed to Monitor the Identified Risks

With every DCO, COBIT links one or more CPs.

> Each IT control objective expands the capabilities of COBIT by providing the practitioner with an additional level of detail. The COBIT IT processes, business requirements and detailed control objectives define what needs to be done to implement an effective control structure. The control practices provide the more detailed how and why needed by management, service providers, end users and control professionals to implement highly specific controls based on an analysis of operational and IT risks [2].

The CPs linked to a specific DCO were, therefore, used as 'drivers' to determine the data and information required to manage a specific DCO (IT risk).

These CPs were also stored in the database, and linked to their relevant DCOs.

Guided by the CPs, a comprehensive set of data-capturing mechanisms were identified and developed to extract and provide the precise data and information required by every CP. Some of these mechanisms were manual, in the sense that they consisted of questionnaires which had to be completed, while other mechanisms were electronic in the sense they extracted data directly from the operational environment.

Data-capturing mechanisms are multifunctional in the sense that a specific mechanism can be used to feed data to different CPs.

At this stage, the database system of our Compliance Management Approach mentioned above consists of the following:

- 62 (generic) DCOs (IT risks);
- the relevant CPs for each DCO;
- a set of data capturing mechanisms for each CP.

7.8.2.3 More on the Data-Capturing Mechanisms

As stated above, the data-capturing mechanisms are manual or electronic. It is important to say more about this distinction between the two ways of capturing information.

Suppose information is needed about the level of Information Security awareness of IT users. There are basically no electronic systems from which this information can be captured, so it has to be done manually by using a questionnaire. The same holds true for determining data about physical security, for example, the closing of access doors, the efficiency of fire extinguisher services, etc.

Such data is, however, not required every day, so doing it once or twice a year by manual means is acceptable.

Therefore, there is one set of identified DCOs (IT risks) for which manual capturing is acceptable, and data capture forms are designed and ready to use when needed. This is called manually captured data.

Suppose on the other hand that information is needed about the configuration of every workstation to determine if any unauthorized changes have been made. In most cases, although this can, in theory, be done manually by inspection, it is not realistic, especially if hundreds of workstations are involved. Furthermore, it is no use finding out after three weeks that a configuration was changed – it may be far too late. Therefore, in this case, the data must be captured from every workstation, on a daily basis, and this can only be done electronically.

Therefore, there is a second set of DCOs (IT risks) which absolutely needs electronic capturing of data. This is called electronically captured data.

It is important to also understand that manually capturing data is always possible because it is done via a manual method. Electronically capturing data is not always possible because the company may not have the required software to capture the data electronically. For example, to capture daily information on workstation configurations, an enterprise-wide desk-top management system needs to be installed. If such a system is not present, that required information may not be available to be captured electronically.

The Methodology to implement the Compliance Management Approach will now be discussed.

7.8.3 The Methodology

The Methodology consists of a number of steps. These steps will now be discussed.

Step 1: A Risk Analysis exercise is scheduled with members of Executive Management, business system owners and other stakeholders

The 62 DCOs in the System database are then taken one by one, and the group is asked to evaluate this DCO as far as its relevance to the company is concerned. The approach taken is to identify (quantify) the risk to the company which will arise if this DCO is not properly controlled and managed. A scale of 0–8 is used. Consensus is reached on each of the 62 DCOs. A spin-off from the exercise is also that very often the attendees become much more aware of and sensitive to IT risks.

The meeting also decided by consensus what cut-off point they want to implement, i.e., look at all risks which got a rating of 5 or higher, or 6 or higher, etc.

Step 2: Because of the structure of the System's database discussed above, immediately after entering the results from the risk analysis exercise into the System (the ratings for each DCO), it is possible to get a precise indication of which CPs are relevant, and more important, which data and information must be captured, using the identified data-capturing mechanisms, to start managing the identified risks.

Step 3: In this step, the electronic data-capturing mechanisms available in the company are investigated. As mentioned above, it may be possible that for an identified DCO, specific electronically captured data is required, but that the company does not have the software available to capture that data. This means that a specific DCO (IT risk) was identified during the Risk Analysis exercise, but the data required to manage that risk is not available.

All identified DCOs and all electronically required data-capturing mechanisms are investigated, and a Managed Risk Profile (MRP) is constructed. This Profile indicates the potential of the company to manage a specific identified DCO (IT risk).

Fig. 7.1 below gives an idea of such an MRP.

This example uses the 21 DCOs from COBIT's DS 5. The first bar indicates that only 36% of the required electronic information to monitor this DCO can be acquired from the company's IT infrastructure. Therefore, although the business had identified this DCO (IT risk) as very important, in the best situation, it is only possible to manage this risk up to a 35% level.

When such an MRP is presented back to Executive Management, it can get a very good idea of what the potential of IT risk management in the company is, and is, in all cases, an eye opener!

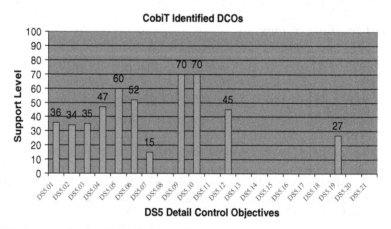

Fig. 7.1 An example of a managed risk profile

Executive Management must now decide whether it wants to accept the 36% level for DS 5.1, or whether it wants to spend money to acquire the necessary IT infrastructure to up the management level to, say, 70% or whatever level. However, it is now made aware of the potential to manage this risk and cannot claim ignorance at a later stage.

The creation of the MRP provides a good insight into the capability of the company to manage the identified risks.

It is, of course, important to get a more frequent view of precisely how these risks are managed. This leads to Step 4.

Step 4: During this step, the available data-capturing mechanisms in the company are activated (used) to extract the required data from the relevant environments (as discussed in 7.8.2.2).

The captured data are then combined in a Report database, using different ways of combining captured data elements, determined by a measurement stack, to provide a report on the risk status of every one of the originally identified risks.

The Report database also keeps track of all previous reports for a specific risk, and provides a picture of how this risk is changing over a time period.

Below are two examples of such reports (Fig. 7.2 and 7.3).

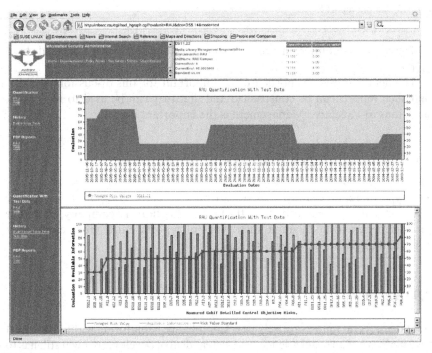

Fig. 7.2 Sample report A

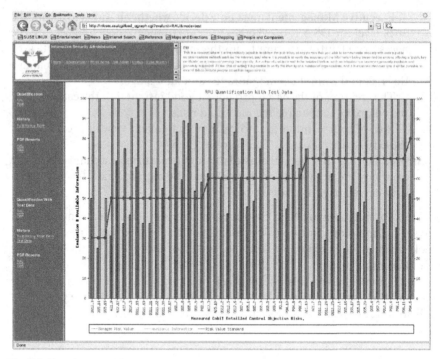

Fig. 7.3 Sample report B

These reports contain information on every one of the risks decided on in Step 1.

The details in these reports are not important for this discussion: the idea that such reports can be constructed and that they can be used to report risk situations to Executive Management is the important aspect.

7.8.4 Reporting to Executive Management

The type of reports shown above can now be used to report to Executive Management and the Board about the IT risk situation in a company. Executive Management will understand such types of reports much more easily than pages and pages of figures and statistics.

7.9 Summary

As stated several times, precisely how Compliance Monitoring within ISG must take place is not an exact science, and a great deal of development will still has to take place.

Nevertheless, the importance of this component within the whole ISG cycle cannot be over-emphasized.

This chapter provides some background and ideas on how this can be done.

References

1. ISO/IEC 27002 (2005). Information Technology – Security Techniques – Code of Practice for Information Security Management. International Organization for Standardization. Available from www.iso.ch
2. COBIT (2005). Control Objectives for Information and Related Technology. Available from ISACA. www.isaca.org

Chapter 8
IT Risk Management

8.1 Introduction

Good Corporate Governance practices determine that a Board and Senior Management must set a clear vision and strategic objectives for their organization. Unfortunately some constraints might hinder the realization of this vision and strategic objectives. These constraints are known as risks.

As the Board and Senior Management are ultimately responsible for the well-being of the organization, they must ensure that all risks are properly addressed. For this reason, Risk Management is definitely their responsibility.

> Risk Management is the process to identify and assess all potential risks as well as introducing controls that should mitigate all these risks to acceptable low levels.

Information and IT are critical to the success of any organization and, therefore, IT risks are also a Senior Management responsibility.

8.2 The History and Essence of Risk

The term *risk* dates back to the seventeenth century when mathematicians calculated the risk of winning or losing when gambling. Risk referred to a combination between probability and magnitude of potential gains and losses. During the eighteenth century, risk still considered both gains and losses and was employed in the marine insurance business. Risk in the study of economics emerged in the nineteenth century. By the twentieth century, a total negative connotation was made when referring to outcomes of risk in engineering and science, with particular reference to the hazards posed by modern technological developments such as in the petro-chemical and nuclear industries.

Today, in most circumstances, risk has two factors associated with it:

a probability or frequency aspect; and
a magnitude of gains or losses (impact) aspect.

Any risk has always some potential *impact* associated with it and also some *probability* or *frequency* aspect. Thus, one should always attempt to determine

S.H. von Solms, R. von Solms, *Information Security Governance*,
DOI 10.1007/978-0-387-79984-1_8, © Springer Science+Business Media, LLC 2009

firstly, what the impact will be if the risk does materialize and secondly, how often (probability or frequency) this risk might materialize. If fire destroys the entire computer centre, the impact will be serious although the probability that it might happen is fairly small. On the other hand, the probability that a malicious software virus might infect some business data is fairly high, but normally the impact is not serious.

To control or mitigate a risk, one normally attempts to attain one of three general outcomes:

- reduce the potential impact or the risk;
- reduce the probability or frequency of the risk; or
- a combination of both of the above.

Risks are normally **controlled or mitigated** by means of the effective selection, implementation and maintenance of suitable security controls, countermeasures or safeguards.

In most cases, whether financial, business or IT-related risks, the objective is to identify related risks and to control or mitigate them to acceptable levels.

8.3 Risk Management and ISO 27002

Pages 3–5 of ISO 27002 [1] have a very explicit discussion on the concept of risk in IT. The following is one part of that discussion:

> It is essential that an organization identifies its security requirements. There are three main sources of security requirements.
>
> One source is derived from assessing risks to the organization, taking into account the organization's overall business strategy and objectives. Through a risk assessment, threats to assets are identified, vulnerability to and likelihood of occurrence is evaluated and potential impact is estimated.

ISO 27002, therefore, sees IT risk analysis as an essential part of Best Practices in IT.

8.4 Risk Management and COBIT

The PO 9 Control Objective (CO) COBIT [2] concentrates totally on Assessing Risk, under the following items:

Business Risk Assessment
Management should establish a systematic risk assessment framework. Such a framework should incorporate a regular assessment of the relevant information risks to the achievement of the business objectives, forming a basis for determining how the risks should be managed to an acceptable level.

Risk Assessment Approach
Management should establish a general risk assessment approach that defines the scope and boundaries, the methodology to be adopted for risk assessments, the responsibilities and the required skills.

Risk Identification
The risk assessment approach should focus on the examination of the essential elements of risk and the cause/effect relationship between them. The essential elements of risk include tangible and intangible assets, asset value, threats, vulnerabilities, safeguards, consequences and likelihood of threat. The risk identification process should include qualitative and, where appropriate, quantitative risk ranking and should obtain input from management brainstorming, strategic planning, past audits and other assessments. The risk assessment should consider business, regulatory, legal, technology, trading partner and human resources risks.

Risk Measurement
The risk assessment approach should ensure that the analysis of risk identification information results in a quantitative and/or qualitative measurement of risk to which the examined area is exposed. The risk acceptance capacity of the organization should also be assessed.

Risk Action Plan
The risk assessment approach should provide for the definition of a risk action plan to ensure that cost-effective controls and security measures mitigate exposure to risks on a continuing basis.

Risk Acceptance
The risk assessment approach should ensure the formal acceptance of the residual risk, depending on risk identification and measurement, organizational policy, uncertainty incorporated in the risk assessment approach itself, and the cost effectiveness of implementing safeguards and controls.

Safeguard Selection
While aiming for a reasonable, appropriate and proportional system of controls and safeguards, controls with the highest return on investment (ROI) and those that provide quick wins should receive first priority. The control system also should balance prevention, detection, correction and recovery measures.

Risk Assessment Commitment
Management should encourage risk assessment as an important tool in providing information in the design and implementation of internal controls, in the definition of the IT strategic plan and in the monitoring and evaluation mechanisms.

COBIT, therefore, also sees Risk Management as a core element of IT Governance.

8.5 Risk Management and Governance

From the discussion above, and from Chapters 1, 2 and 3 of this book, it should be clear that Risk Management is a very comprehensive process. Ultimately, it is the responsibility of the Board and Executive Management. All risks that could possibly have a negative effect on the well-being of the organization (if and once they materialize) are definitely the responsibility of management. Thus, all levels of organizational management should be involved in the process of Risk Management.

Another important factor is that it is imperative that information and IT-related risks be managed in an integrated manner with business risks, as most business processes are nowadays totally integrated with IT and absolutely dependent on information.

If information and IT are critical to the well-being of the organization, then Risk Management is, without any doubt, a management issue, even at Board and Executive Management levels

8.6 Definitions, Terminology and Relationships

Risk Management and its underlying aspects and terms are applicable and used in many disciplines. Business risks, financial risks and many other risks related to other disciplines need to be managed along with information and information technology-related risks. Therefore, as risk-related terms are used in many different disciplines, it is important to list and define a number of terms to be used in the discussion of Risk Management.

Although the following list is not complete, most of the terms used in the rest of this chapter will be described briefly (descriptions mostly from ISO 27002):

- **asset** – anything that has value to an organization;
- **threat** – a potential cause of an unwanted incident, which may result in harm to a system or organization;
- **vulnerability** – a weakness of an asset or group of assets that can be exploited by one or more threats;
- **risk** – combination of the probability of an event and its consequence;
- **control** – means of managing risk, including policies, procedures, guidelines, practices or organizational structures, which can be of administrative, technical, management, or legal nature. (Control is also used as a synonym for safeguard or countermeasure);
- **residual risk** – the remaining risk after controls have been implemented;
- **risk analysis** – systematic use of information to identify sources and to estimate the risk;
- **risk evaluation** – process of comparing the estimated risk against given risk criteria to determine the significance of the risk;
- **risk assessment** – overall process of risk analysis and risk evaluation;
- **risk treatment** – process of selection and implementation of measures to modify risk;
- **risk management** – coordinated activities to direct and control an organization with regard to risk.

Most of these terms relate to one another in one or other way. The following are some descriptions of these interrelationships.

An *asset* is threatened by one or more *threats*. Normally, a *threat* can only influence an *asset* through some *vulnerability* in the protection of the asset. A *risk* normally constitutes an asset, a threat and a vulnerability, as depicted in Fig. 8.1.

The extent or size of the *risk* (as graphically demonstrated in Fig. 8.2) is determined by a combination of the *impact* it will have on the *asset* as well as the

Fig. 8.1 Components
constituting a risk

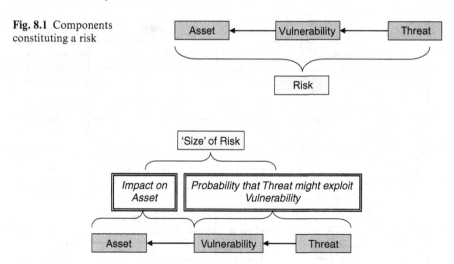

Fig. 8.2 The 'size' of a risk

frequency or *probability* that some *threat* might exploit some *vulnerability*. (Thus, the size of a risk is determined by a combination of the impact it will have on the asset, if it materializes, as well as the frequency or probability that some threat might exploit some vulnerability to influence the asset)

The size of a risk is determined by a combination of the impact it will have on the asset, if it materializes, as well as the frequency or probability that some threat might exploit a vulnerability to influence the asset.

Security *controls* are identified and introduced to mitigate or control a risk. In general, the objective of any control is to either reduce the *impact* (that the threat might have on the asset once it materializes) or to reduce the *frequency* or *probability* that the threat might exploit some *vulnerability*. The *probability* normally refers to a combination of the *threat* and the *vulnerability*.

As most *risks* cannot be controlled or mitigated fully, some *residual risk* is normally left. If the residual risk proves to be small enough, it is normally accepted by the organization.

More than one threat may potentially exploit a single vulnerability (see Threats 1 & 2 above). A single threat may potentially exploit more than one vulnerability (see Threat 4 in Fig. 8.3 above).

The introduction of suitable, effective controls should reduce the probability that the threat may exploit some vulnerability or reduce the impact if the threat does find a way to exploit a vulnerability.

Threat 3 (as per Fig. 8.3) has got a good chance to exploit a vulnerability and have an adverse impact on some assets. This scenario constitutes an uncontrolled risk.

The probability that a threat may exploit some vulnerabilities and have a negative impact on some assets can normally not be nullified. For this reason,

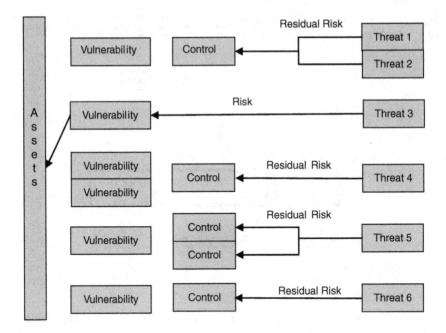

Fig. 8.3 Controlling risks

some residual risk will normally remain; however, this residual risk must be acceptable to management.

Taking all relationships and principles mentioned and illustrated above into account, the question arises:

> Which controls and at what level of detail would be adequate to reduce risks to such levels that the residual risks are acceptable to management?

To answer this question, it is obvious that all major risks need to be identified, listed and evaluated. Suitable controls then need to be identified and implemented. All of this might seem very easy and straightforward, but this is, in fact, not the case. A series of structured processes are normally used to identify, evaluate and treat all major risks. The following is a brief description of the processes involved:

The terminology and relationships, as depicted and described in Fig. 8.4 above are according to ISO 27002.

Other sources might use different terms and relationships, for example:

- Some sources refer to process 3 (Risk Treatment) as Risk Management ;
- Some sources refer to process 5 (Risk Management) as Management of Risk;
- Some sources refer to process 4 (Risk Assessment) as Risk Analysis;
- Some sources also refer to Risk Prioritization, when risks are prioritized according to the extent or 'size' of the risk;

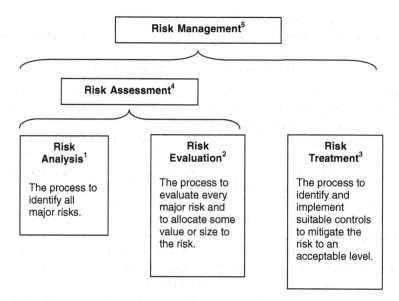

Fig. 8.4 Risk-related terminology and relationships

- Some sources refer to Risk Analysis to include: risk identification, risk estimation & risk evaluation.

Important: Although the terminology might differ from one source to another, the basic process remains largely the same.

The process to identify and implement controls (risk treatment) remains contentious and, to some extent, subjective. Suitable controls are to be identified (and implemented) based mainly on the results of the risk-evaluation exercise. Thus, the size or potential extent of the risk might be the only indicator to assist in this regard. Controls can be selected from a Best Practice (like ISO 27002), or it can be developed in-house or identified from other sources.

It is important to note that any risk analysis exercise is conducted mainly to assist in identifying and motivating suitable controls.

8.7 Processes that Constitute Risk Management

Risk Management is defined above as "those coordinated activities to direct and control an organization with regard to risk." (Remember, the objective of Risk Management is to ultimately identify the most suitable set of controls to mitigate risks to an acceptable level.)

From this definition, it can be deduced that Risk Management consists of a number of 'coordinated activities'. Basically, three major activities can be highlighted. They are:

- Identify all major risks (risk analysis);
- Evaluate all these risks – allocating some value or size to each risk (risk evaluation);
- Select suitable controls to mitigate risks (risk treatment).

Identifying risks that need to be controlled can follow various ways and techniques. Some formal and informal or a combination of techniques can be used to identify risks that need to be controlled.

No matter what technique (formal or informal) is followed, the idea is to identify, at least, the asset (as well as the potential impact associated with the risk), as well as the threat (as well as the probability) associated with every risk and, preferably, some vulnerability as well.

To identify a risk, some asset (with the potential impact the risk might cause if it manifests), as well as a threat (with the probability to manifests) and, preferably, some vulnerability as well.

Evaluating risks is the process to assign some value to each risk. Based on these risk values, risks can be prioritized and ordered. This should provide an indication of which risks are the biggest and should be addressed first.

Two approaches are normally used to evaluate risks: these are quantitative and qualitative. Quantitative approaches normally utilize 'real' values, like monetary values and/or probability values. Qualitative approaches tend to use values on a scale, for example, Low, Medium and High or values on a Lickert Scale of 1–5. A combination of the quantitative and qualitative approaches can also be used.

No matter which approach is used to evaluate risks (quantitative or qualitative), the objective is to calculate or assign some value to each risk to enable some risk prioritization to determine which risks are the biggest and need to be treated first.

Selecting controls is the process to identify and implement the most suitable set of controls to mitigate each risk to an acceptable level. Once the identified controls are introduced, the residual risk should be small enough that management may accept it.

Controls can be identified from a variety of sources. A very common manner to identify controls nowadays is to use international Best Practices, such as ISO 27002.

Remember, ultimately, the objective of Risk Management is to identify controls. Risk identification and evaluation are processes to assist in identifying the most suitable set of controls.

8.8 Risk Analysis, Estimation and Treatment

8.8.1 Risk Analysis

Risk analysis is primarily the process of identifying all risks. This be done in a formal, structured way, or some more informal ways can be followed.

To identify and analyze risks in a structured way, a more 'bottom-up' approach is followed. The individual assets, threats and vulnerabilities are identified. This is followed by some process where assets are related to threats and risks are deduced. Thus, by successfully relating some asset to some threat, a risk is identified. This process of comparing all assets to threats should result in all potential risks being identified.

Example 8.1

If a laptop computer is identified as an asset, and theft identified as a threat, then the **theft of laptop computers** can be deduced as a risk.

One the other hand, a more informal approach to identify and analyze risks can also be used. This tends to be more a 'top-down' approach as the risk is normally identified and then needs to be 'analyzed' to identify the underlying asset and threat.

Example 8.2

A Manager states that he/she is very concerned about the fact that some client credit card numbers, stored in the company database, can possibly be compromised. In this case, **theft of information** (credit card numbers) can be identified as the risk. As the asset is analyzed, information is identified as the asset and theft as the threat.

Normally, a combination of formal and informal approaches is used to identify all risks.

8.8.2 Risk Estimation

Risk estimation is the process to determine some value of the 'size' of the risk. As mentioned earlier, two aspects contribute towards risk estimation. These are:

1. The *impact* the threat might have on the asset if it materializes; and
2. The *probability* that the threat might exploit some vulnerability.

To assign a value to the risk, some values must be assigned to the *impact* as well as the *probability*. These two values will eventually constitute the size of the risk. These values assigned to the impact and to the probability (or frequency) are normally done in one of two ways: either a *quantitative* or a *qualitative* approach is followed.

Quantitative approach to risk estimation

This approach tends to use real values, for example, monetary values to express the impact and frequency per year to express the probability value. If the monetary impact value is multiplied by the annual probability value, an Annual Loss Expectancy (ALE) value can be calculated for that specific risk.

Example 8.3

Take the risk identified in Example 8.1 above. A value of R30 000 is assigned to the impact if the laptop is stolen. It is decided that on average two laptops (from a total of 50 company laptops) are stolen every year and therefore a probability (frequency) value of 2. An Annual Loss Expectancy (ALE) is calculated by multiplying the impact value and the probability value. Thus, an Annual Loss Expectancy of R60 000 (R30 000 × 2) is calculated for the risk of laptop computers getting stolen.

Once an ALE is calculated for all risks, the risks can be prioritized from the largest to the smallest.

Qualitative approach to risk estimation

This approach tends to use qualitative values. Typical examples are either Lickert Scale values (from 1–5), descriptive values such as: the impact will be Minor, Significant, Major or Disastrous, or probability values such as: hardly ever, seldom, regularly, often or very often.

These qualitative values are then used to either calculate (impact multiplied by probability) a risk value or to look up a risk value from some look-up table.

ISO 13335 [3] proposes the following tables (Tables 8.1a and 8.1b) to assign impact and probability values and then to look up a risk value.

Example 8.4

Take the risk identified in Example 8.1 above. An impact value of 2 can be assigned to losing the laptop. If the threat of theft is estimated as Low and the vulnerability of the theft of laptop computers is estimated as Medium, then a Risk value of 3 is looked up from the risk table.

Thus, from above it can be seen that risks can be allocated some value by either using quantitative or qualitative approaches. This does not really matter, as the main objective of risk estimation is to assign some value to each risk and

Table 8.1a Impact table

Impact value	Description	Ranking
R0–R10 000	Low impact	1
R10 001–R100 000	Noticeable impact	2
R100 001–R500 000	Severe impact	3
R500 001–	Critical impact	4

Adapted from ISO 13335 [3].

Table 8.1b Risk table

	Threat	L	L	L	M	M	M	H	H	H
Impact value	Vulnerability	L	M	H	L	M	H	L	M	H
1		1	2	3	2	3	4	3	4	5
2		2	3	4	3	4	5	4	5	6
3		3	4	5	4	5	6	5	6	7
4		4	5	6	5	6	7	6	7	8

to be able to prioritize risks from the largest to the smallest. This prioritization is used to determine which risks should receive the most attention when risk treatment is applied.

Even though risk estimation can be very subjective, as a great deal of guess-work goes into estimation, it does provide some indication as to which risks are the largest and which are the smaller ones.

8.8.3 Risk Treatment

Risk treatment is the process to identify suitable controls to mitigate each risk to some acceptable level.

According to ISO 27002:

For each of the risks identified following the risk assessment, a risk treatment decision needs to be made. Possible options for risk treatment include:

a. applying appropriate controls to reduce the risks;
b. knowingly and objectively accepting risks, providing they clearly satisfy the organization's policy and criteria for risk acceptance;
c. avoiding risks by not allowing actions that would cause the risks to occur;
d. transferring the associated risks to other parties, e.g., insurers or suppliers.

For those risks where the risk treatment decision has been to apply appropriate controls, these controls should be selected and implemented to meet the requirements identified by a risk assessment. Controls should ensure that risks are reduced to an acceptable level taking into account:

a. requirements and constraints of national and international legislation and regulations;
b. organizational objectives;
c. operational requirements and constraints;
d. cost of implementation and operation in relation to the risks being reduced and remaining proportional to the organization's requirements and constraints;
e. the need to balance the investment in implementation and operation of controls against the harm likely to result from security failures.

Controls can be selected from this standard (ISO 27002) or from other control sets, or new controls can be designed to meet the specific needs of the organization.

8.9 Risk Management

Risk Management, following a formalized, structured approach normally includes, among others, the following steps (see Fig. 8.5):

Risk Management – a formalized, structured approach

1) Risk Assessment

   a) Risk Analysis

      i) Assets

         (1) Asset identification (identify all important and valuable assets – both tangible and non-tangible)

         (2) Value each asset (determine possible impact if asset is compromised)

      ii) Threats

         (1) Threat identification (identify all possible threats that may influence any of the assets in a negative way)

         (2) Threat assessment (determine the likelihood or probability of threat manifestation)

      iii) Vulnerabilities

         (1) Vulnerability assessment (determine the degree of weaknesses that might be exploited)

   b) Risk Evaluation

      i) Determine, calculate or look-up risk value or size
      ii) Prioritize risks according to risk value

2. Risk Treatment

   a) Identify suitable controls to satisfactorily mitigate risks
   b) Implement identified controls

Fig. 8.5 Risk Management - a formalized, structured approach

8.10 IT Risk and the Management Levels

It was mentioned in the Introduction that the Board and Executive Management are ultimately responsible for managing all risks that may have a serious effect on the organization.

One question that can be asked is:

How are the various levels of Management (Strategic, Tactical and Operational) involved in the exercise of Risk Management?

One approach that can be followed is to involve the upper two levels in the more informal risk assessment exercises.

8.10.1 Strategic Management Level

Possible involvement of Executive Management

Executive Management can actively participate by indicating which major information-related risks (worries) bother management.

The following question might be asked to members of Executive Management:

As far as business information and information technology are concerned, what worries you the most? Something that might happen and really put the organization at risk?

Example 8.5

In answering the question posed above, the CEO states: *"Since I read in the newspaper about the CEO that was sued for negligence because more than a thousand client credit card numbers were compromised through some hacking attempt and published on the WWW, I am really worried as we also store client credit card numbers."*

Remember, answers from open questions, as posed above, need to be interpreted, and the underlying asset (and associated impact) as well as the threat and its probability and vulnerabilities need to be identified.

8.10.2 Tactical Management Level

Possible involvement of Middle Management

Managers at the Tactical Level can be involved in an informal manner in some Event/Impact Analysis to identify possible risks.

Event/Impact Analysis is conducted by asking specific questions. These questions can ideally be asked to Management.

Questions to Management:

What are your fears about risks that might **impact** the organization as far as the following are concerned –
  Adverse press coverage
  Loss of income
  Inability to continue with some business processes
  Unforeseen costs
  Legal action against organization or employees
  Dissatisfied customers?

Which of these **events,** and in which way, do you think might have a negative impact on the organization –
  Theft
  Acts of God, vandalism and terrorism
  Fraud
  IT failure
  Hacking
  Denial of service
  Disclosure
  Legal?

Following the answers from questions posed above, risks can again be identified. Question 1 above already identifies the impact and Question 2 the threats that will be involved in the individual risks.

An Event/Impact Analysis can be very effective in identifying risks and management can be involved in the analysis.

8.10.3 Operational Management Level

On the Operational Level, more formal risk assessment techniques are used. More information on these detailed risk assessment techniques does not form part of this chapter.

8.11 Summary

Risk Management is core to IT and Information Security Governance because in order to properly protect something, one must know both what it is one is protecting and against what.

References

1. ISO/IEC 27002 (2005). Information Technology – Security Techniques – Code of Practice for Information Security Management. International Organization for Standardization. Available from www.iso.ch
2. COBIT (2005). Control Objectives for Information and Related Technology. Available from ISACA. www.isaca.org
3. ISO/IEC 13335 (2004). Information Technology – Security Techniques – Management of Information and Communications Technology Security – Part 1: Concepts and Models for Information and Communications Technology Security Management. International Organization for Standardization. Available from www.iso.ch

Chapter 9
Organizing the Information Security Function

9.1 Introduction

In any company, the way Information Security is organized is very important. All Best Practice documents underline this aspect.

Traditionally, and in many cases still today, the Information Security function is seen as an integral part of the IT function, and is usually totally contained in the IT function.

More recent thinking has underlined the fact that such a way of organizing Information Security is an oversimplification, and several newer models are emerging which differ from this traditional view.

Today, it is realized that there must be at least two components to Information Security organization – a component which looks after the day-to-day operational aspects related to it, and a component which is responsible for the compliance monitoring function as introduced in Chapter 7.

This chapter basically follows this last approach.

This chapter returns to the aspect of compliance, discussed in Chapter 7, and makes a distinction between Compliance Management and Operational Management of Information Security. Both will be briefly discussed, and then a model will be provided as to how these functions and, therefore, Information Security as a whole can be organized in a company.

However, before that, it is necessary to see what the two driving Best Practice documents introduced earlier, say about this aspect.

9.2 ISO 27002 on Organization

Clause 6 of ISO 27002 [1] is titled 'Organization of Information Security', and contains guidelines on this aspect. The content of the clause is repeated below:

6 ORGANIZATION OF INFORMATION SECURITY

S.H. von Solms, R. von Solms, *Information Security Governance*,
DOI 10.1007/978-0-387-79984-1_9, © Springer Science+Business Media, LLC 2009

This clause does not say very much about the formal way of organization, but emphasizes the importance of this component of our Model in general.

9.3 COBIT on Organization

The high-level process of PO 4 in COBIT [2] covers several aspects related to the organization of the IT function in a company. While this relates to IT in general, only Control Objective PO 4.8 mentions security specifically.

9.4 Compliance and Operational Management of Information Security

The rest of the discussion in this chapter is strongly based on the paper; Information Security Governance – Compliance Management vs Operational Management [3].

The essential importance of the discipline of Information Security in any company using any type of IT infrastructure is no longer disputed by anyone today, and is accepted as an integral part of managing any IT environment.

As stated in Chapter 3, Information Security Governance (ISG) is now accepted as an integral part of good ITG and Corporate Governance.

Therefore, the position of Information Security Manager (ISM) has become an established position in all companies, making the person occupying this position responsible for the full Information Security programme in the company.

Today, very few companies, if any, do not have such a position – in smaller companies this person may have other responsibilities too, while in large companies the person usually has a whole department supporting this position.

The ISM is, in general, responsible for all aspects related to Information Security in the company.

However, external forces and developments are forcing a redefinition of the all-encompassing role of an ISM.

This chapter reviews the activities of a company's ISM and the organization of the Information Security function in general.

Because of the wider use of IT in companies, and new risks arising because of the use of IT – risks like the Internet, WWW, wireless networks and instant messaging – a wide range of policies and procedures concerning the use of IT by all users is created by companies to ensure that IT is used in a secure way.

Today, these types of policies are regularly demanded by internationally accepted best practices for Information Security Management, and have, therefore, become an essential requirement for good ITG, and, therefore, for good Corporate Governance.

The importance of ensuring compliance with these policies, and enforcing the proper and consistent use of them has become as important as ensuring that the necessary technical security measures are in place.

The two aspects mentioned in the last two paragraphs above – that of policies and procedures, and the compliance enforcement of such policies and procedures, are central to the concept of ISG, as indicated by the preceding chapters in this book.

The definition of ISG provided in Chapter 3 states:

> ISG consists of the management commitment and leadership, organizational structures, user awareness and commitment, policies, procedures, processes, technologies and compliance enforcement mechanisms, all working together to ensure that the confidentiality, integrity and availability (CIA) of the company's electronic assets (data, information, software, hardware, people etc.) are maintained at all times.

Information Security Management, as traditionally defined, and as presently handled in most companies, covers a part of the wider concept of ISG. It addresses most, if not all aspects related to Operational Information Security Management, discussed in the next paragraph, as well as many aspects related to the creation of policies, procedures, etc. However, the aspect of compliance monitoring and enforcement, as required by ISG, has not really yet become part of the traditional role of Information Security Management.

This is precisely where the (traditional) role of Information Security Management has changed significantly over the last couple of years – a distinct difference between Information Security Compliance Management and Information Security Operational Management has become clear. This distinction had always been there, but was probably not as clear and defined as it has now become.

This aspect had already been introduced in Chapter 7 where the aspects related to compliance were discussed. This chapter argues that this distinction has become so essential to ISG that it should now start receiving the necessary attention to separate these two ISG concepts and reflect that in the way Information Security is organized in a company.

ISG must, therefore, be seen as consisting of two separate parts – one for Information Security Operational Management, which has always been there, and Information Security Compliance Management, which has also always been there, but which has traditionally been tightly integrated with Operational Management.

Proper ISG demands that these two be totally separated. This will be motivated in the rest of this chapter.

9.5 Information Security Operational Management

This part or dimension of ISG has always been understood, and is, to a certain extent, well defined.

Activities included in this dimension are, for example:

- Logical access control management, i.e., the real actions of adding to, changing and deleting user access rights from access control lists, etc;
- Identification and authentication management, i.e., the real actions of adding to, changing and deleting from the user ID database and password files;
- Firewall management in terms of configuring firewalls with the authorized access rights, connecting workstations to LANS and the Internet, etc;
- Virus and malicious software management, i.e., installing and updating anti-virus software;
- Handling anti-virus and related types of security incidents;
- Setting and updating the security settings and configurations of workstations and servers;
- Ensuring availability through UPS systems;
- Ensuring backups and secure storage of backups;
- and several others.

These activities are crucial and essential to ensure any IT environment against any risks which may affect the confidentiality, integrity and availability of the company's electronic assets.

Traditionally, these actions had been seen as representing Information Security Management, creating the misconception that it is actually a technical job and best left to the technicians.

Fortunately, this image has changed significantly, and the non-technical activities of Information Security Management have found their rightful place.

These non-technical activities include, for example:

- The creation of Information Security policies and procedures
- The creation of Awareness programmes to make all users aware of the risks involved in using IT systems, and their responsibilities towards mediating the IT risks
- The compliance enforcement mechanisms to ensure compliance with all policies and procedures are enforced, and to ensure that IT risks are properly managed and meditated

These non-technical activities, together with the technical activities mentioned above, are today, more or less, generally accepted as making up Information Security Management.

However, the last bullet point above, that of the creation of methods and systems to ensure and measure compliance with relevant policies and procedures, is becoming more and more important in the light of good ISG, good ITG and good Corporate Governance.

Compliance measuring and enforcement have become pivotal to good ISG in general. Chapter 7 discussed this in more detail.

This aspect, which is closely linked to Chapter 7, is further investigated in the next paragraph.

9.6 Information Security Compliance Management

The fact that an unenforced policy is not worth the paper it is written on, is a generally accepted fact.

In all cases, including that of Information Security, it is essential to measure and enforce compliance.

Furthermore, today, good ITG and Corporate Governance demand that risks should be lowered, and properly managed, and an essential part of such risk mediation is to enforce compliance.

Within general ISG, the role and activity of compliance measurement and enforcement had become a very important component of general IT Risk Management in the company. This was extensively discussed in Chapter 7.

This, in itself, is also not new, because the roles of Internal and External IT audits have always been to identify areas of risk in the use of IT, and to report on the level of compliance to relevant policies, etc.

Today's severe dependence on IT systems do not, however, allow the luxury of a once-a-year Internal IT audit report – a day-to-day compliance measurement and enforcement activity is essential.

This has lead to the growing field of Managed Information Security, where, often in an outsourced mode, many activities are monitored in real time, and reported to the relevant people to take action.

General Information Security compliance measurement and enforcement include, however, more than what is provided by such Managed Information Security services.

Activities which must be managed as far as compliance is concerned include:

- The level to which previously identified IT risks are managed and mediated;
- The level of Information Security awareness of users;
- The availability, completeness and comprehensiveness of Information Security policies, procedures and standards;
- The level of compliance to such policies, procedures and standards;
- The impact on the IT risk position of the company when policies are not complied with;

- The compliance with regulatory, legal and statutory requirements;
- Software licensing issues;
- and others.

The first bullet point above, that of monitoring the level to which previously identified IT risks are managed and mediated, is especially important. Such levels of compliance must be regularly reported to Executive Management and the Board to allow them to exercise their responsibilities as far as Governance is concerned. This type of high-level reporting is (usually) not done by the Managed Information Security services referred to above.

It is precisely here that a separation between Operational and Compliance Management of Information Security becomes essential.

This will be discussed in more detail in the next paragraph.

9.7 Compliance Management versus Operational Management

The separation of duties has always been a cornerstone of proper management. That is why the Internal Audit department is separate from the Finance department, and why the Audit department should act objectively and independently.

For the same reason an IT Audit is not a function of the IT Department.

The same aspect is relevant to the aspects of Information Security discussed above.

A proper Information Security Compliance programme (department/section) should not be part of the Information Security operational programme, precisely because of the aspects related to separation of duties mentioned above.

If the Operational Information Security department has to measure how well it complies with relevant policies and procedures, and how successful its risk mediation efforts are, the results may not always be objective and true.

For the same reasons the IT Audit Department is separated from the IT Department, so too the Information Security Compliance Management function must be separated from the Information Security Operational Management function.

This separation will become a very important aspect of good IT Governance.

This, of course, means that the Information Security Compliance Management function must be housed either as a totally separate department or section, or hosted by some other department or section, for example, Audit or Risk Management.

9.8 The Information Security Operational Management Function

The Information Security Operational Management department is what is known as the 'traditional' Information Security department, performing the functions as discussed in Paragraph 9.3 above.

The positioning of this department can be depicted as represented in Fig. 9.1:

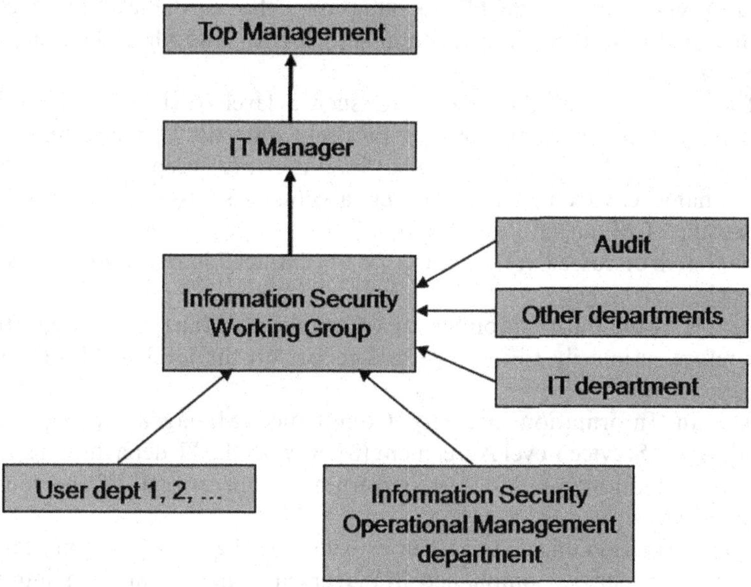

Fig. 9.1 Information security operational management

This department is responsible for the type of operations as discussed in Paragraph 9.5 above. This department reports to the IT Manager, who chairs the Information Security Operational Working Group. This Working Group brings together the technical Information Security requirements and interests of a lot of stakeholders, including User departments, the IT department itself, the Audit department and other relevant departments.

This Committee reports via the IT Manager to Executive Management.

9.9 The Information Security Compliance Management function

Having now, in previous paragraphs, made a case for a separate and objectively independent Information Security Compliance Management function, the positioning of this function must be investigated.

For the Information Security Compliance Management department to properly perform its task, it needs information and data. This data can come from different sources, for example:

- data extracted from the operational IT environment;
- data acquired through interviews, questionnaires, etc;
- data acquired through tests and other experimental mechanisms;
- data and information gathered by some compliance management system as discussed in Chapter 7;
- other data.

All these forms of data must then be consolidated as necessary, and interpreted to reflect the present IT risk situation – that is, the level to which the present IT operations mediate or contain the IT risks, and where the company is still exposed.

Of course, to be able to 'calculate' such a level of risk compliance and exposure, a reference framework for precisely what the IT risks are, to what level should they be managed, to what level they are accepted or transferred, and to what level Executive Management accepts these risks, is required. Let us call this our IT Managed Risk Profile.

The system discussed in Paragraph 7.8 of Chapter 7 is an example of such an approach.

The role of the Information Security Compliance Management department is, therefore, primarily to monitor and report on the level of IT risk in the company.

Such an Information Security Compliance Management department should have a Service Level Agreement (SLA) with the IT department specifying the information and data required from the operational IT environment on a daily basis.

This information and data is then provided by the IT department, and the Information Security Compliance Management department then interprets this, and other information and data, to create the relevant Risk Compliance profiles which are used to report to Executive Management, the Audit Committee and the Board.

The Information Security Compliance Management department must, therefore, have a rather direct reporting line high up in the company, for example, to the Audit and/or Executive Committees.

9.10 An Example of the Compliance Management Function

Many of the aspects discussed above can be illustrated by using an example.

Suppose that, during a risk analysis exercise, it was determined that unauthorized software causes a very high risk for the company, and Executive Management has decided that this risk must be managed and lowered as much as possible.

1. The **risk** to be managed and mediated is, therefore, that of unauthorized software on the company's IT systems.
2. Information Security Operational Management will implement countermeasures to mediate the risk. Usually it will consist of installing anti-virus software on all servers and workstations.
3. Installing such anti-virus countermeasures does not always mean that the risk is totally mediated.
4. In some way, as part of IT Governance, it must be determined how well the risk itself is managed, and this must be reported to Executive

Management. Management, on this level, is not interested in how many virus attacks were reported, how many patches were installed, etc. It wants a simple and straightforward idea of how well the specific risk is managed and controlled.

5. Information Security Compliance Management must now determine what information it needs to report on the specific risk, get that information, and create a report to Executive Management which details the risk management level.

6. Suppose the Information Security Compliance Management section decides it needs the following to monitor the specific risk:

   a) The specified configuration of every server and workstation;
   b) The authorized set of software allowed to run on every server and workstation;
   c) A daily report on the actual software running on every server and workstation;
   d) A discrepancy list for every workstation indicating any diversion between the authorized list and the actual list.

   With this last list, it can make some conclusions about the way the specific risk (1 above) is being controlled

7. The Compliance section now specifies in its service level agreement with the Operational Section that the information in a) to d) above must be supplied every morning. From this information, an IT Risk Compliance Profile for this specific risk is compiled and used for reporting to Executive Management.

Compliance with different relevant policies can also be determined from this information.

The independence between the different sections also becomes clear from this example. If the information in (a)–(d) is not correct, wrong conclusions can be drawn.

Information Security Compliance Management must be separated from Information Security Operational Management for the sake of good Governance.

9.11 The Information Security Compliance Management Function

Figure 9.2 shows an Information Security Compliance Management section (department), performing the functions as discussed in Paragraph 9.6 above.

This department reports to the IT Risk Manager, who chairs the IT Risk Management Committee. This IT Risk Management Committee, where the Information Security Compliance Management department is also represented, has representatives from different User Departments.

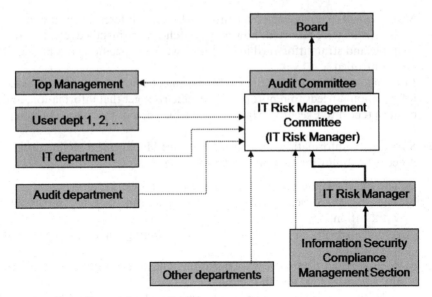

Fig. 9.2 Information security compliance management

The IT Risk Management Committee is a sub-committee of the Audit Committee, and reports through it directly to the Board.

9.12 Putting It All Together

The following diagram now indicates how the full Information Security function can be organized in a company (Fig. 9.3):

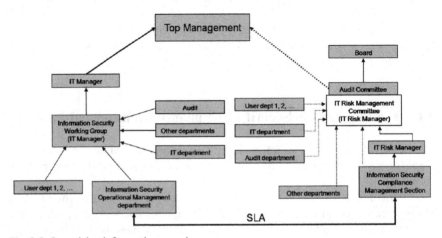

Fig. 9.3 Organizing information security governance

9.13 Summary

This chapter distinguished between Operational and Compliance Management of Information Security and provides an organizational structure which caters for these two forms of management.

The next chapter investigates the aspect of Information Security Awareness.

References

1. ISO/IEC 27002 (2005). Information Technology – Security Techniques – Code of Practice for Information Security Management. International Organization for Standardization. Available from www.iso.ch
2. COBIT (2005). Control Objectives for Information and Related Technology. Available from ISACA. www.isaca.org
3. Von Solms, SH (2005) Information Security Governance – Compliance Management vs Operational Management. Computers & Security, 24(6), 443–447

Chapter 10
Information Security Education, Training and Awareness

10.1 Introduction

Information is the lifeblood of most companies today. Anything that is this important to an organization needs:

- the attention of the Board and
- to be protected properly.

The Board should ensure that a sound Information Security Management System (ISMS) is in place the adequately protect the information resources of the organization.

On the other hand, it is generally accepted today that the protection of the information assets of an organization is the responsibility of ALL employees. Everybody that has access to, communicates, uses, or stores copies of company information must assist in the holistic process of protecting this important organizational asset. These include all users that have access to any organizational information system (end-users), management, IT staff, contract workers and third party companies.

Most company information is nowadays captured, stored, processed and communicated through one or other electronic means. BUT, much of the critical company information is also faxed, photocopied, printed on paper or resides in employees' heads, etc. Furthermore, this valuable company information may be highly mobile as copies of it might be stored on laptop computers, PDAs, cell phones and other highly transportable equipment that can be stolen or lost.

Thus, it is very important today that all 'information workers' should be knowledgeable and be able to play an active role in the protection of valuable company assets.

Example 10.1:

> Every normal household today has got a number of <u>valuables</u> that reside in the house that need to be protected. For this reason, a number of <u>security controls</u> are identified and introduced in every house. These might include: locks to all doors leading to outside the house, a security gate or even an electronic alarm system.

These security controls will prove to be totally useless if the doors and security gates are not properly locked and the alarm system not activated when the house is left. Thus, the operational procedures that support the physical (locks) and technical (alarm system) controls must be obeyed and followed meticulously by everybody living in that home.

Exactly the same situation can be extrapolated onto every company as far as the protection of valuable information assets is concerned.

10.2 Management Components of Information Protection

To adequately protect and secure the continuous safety of information assets, all three organizational management levels must be involved.

Typically these three management levels are involved as follows:

1. At the Strategic Level, an Information Security vision should be defined that should be formalized in *policy*.
2. At the Tactical Level, the required Information Security controls and technologies need to be identified, implemented and maintained. These controls (mostly technology oriented) typically form company security *standards*.
3. To ensure that all organizational Information Security controls and technologies are functioning effectively, it is imperative that proper *procedures, guidelines and practices* for all users of information are devised.

This can be summarized by the following Fig. 10.1:

Executive and senior management devise policies, information technology and security management, determine company security standards and controls, and users of information must follow these practices, guidelines and procedures.

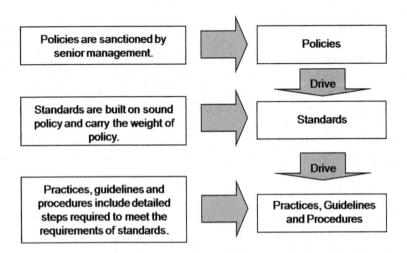

Fig. 10.1 Policies, standards, practices, guidelines and procedures (Adapted from [1])

Policies, *technology* and *people* form the three critical components in the effective protection of information.

10.3 Target Audiences for Security Education, Training and Awareness

As seen from the previous section, all three management levels should play an active and critical role in the effective protection of company information.

1. Strategic Level

    The Board and Executive Management should realize that information and associated information and communication technologies are critical to all modern organizations. ICT is not merely an enabling technology anymore, but plays an integrated, pervasive role in most business processes in driving the business forward.

    Every Board should realize that it is part of their Corporate Governance duties today to ensure that information and the associated IT is properly governed and secured. This duty is normally performed through the setting of IT and Information Security visions and ensuring that company policies are defined and implemented to meet this set of visions. This exact issue was discussed in detail in earlier chapters.

2. Tactical Level

    As Executive and Senior Management define Information Security policies, it is important that these policies are implemented in practical terms. Some IT and Information Security specialists should 'interpret' these policies and identify, implement and maintain suitable security controls to protect company information assets as per associated policies.

    These identified security controls can be physical, technical, managerial and/or operational in nature. Also, these security controls form company standards, as indicated in the figure in the previous section.

3. Operational Level

    As mentioned in the Introduction, almost all Information Security controls are dependent on operational procedures, guidelines or practices to function effectively. For this reason, it is imperative that an extensive set of Information Security procedures, guidelines and practices are drafted and, in an appropriate way, conveyed to all users of information and IT in the organization.

    Thus, all information workers (for example, everybody who has a user ID and password to any company information system) must be made aware (and trained) of the Information Security policy as well as the associated procedures, guidelines and practices. This will enable all information workers (end-users) to actively participate in the effective protection of information- related assets in the organization.

As Information Security-related knowledge, expertise and skills are required by various parties at different organizational levels for different reasons, the emphasis of this chapter is on the latter grouping discussed above, that of the typical end-users in the organization. It must be noted that all levels of management, together with all IT specialists in an organization, also form part of the end-user grouping as all of them make use of company information systems.

Everybody in the organization that has a user ID and password to log onto any company system can be deemed an information worker or end-user and needs to be made aware of Information Security procedures and guidelines and also be trained to effectively execute the associated practices.

10.4 Information Security Education, Training and Awareness (SETA)

Information Security Education, Training and Awareness should be extensions of the general knowledge that employees already have to do their jobs. The objective is to teach each of them to do their jobs securely.

The objectives of a SETA Programme are to:

- Improve awareness of the importance and need to protect organizational information resources;
- Acquire the necessary skills and know-how to do their jobs more securely;
- Create an understanding and insight into why it is important to protect organizational information assets.

It is important that a clear differentiation is made between Awareness, Training and Education. The following table provides some information in this regard (Table 10.1).

Table 10.1 Differentiation between awareness, training and education

	Awareness	Training	Education
Attribute	What	How	Why
Level	Information	Knowledge	Insight
Objective	Alert to	Skill	Understanding
Teaching method	Media	Practical Instruction	Theoretical Instruction
	• Videos	• Lecture	• Seminar
	• Newsletters	• Workshop	• Literature study
	• Posters	• Hands-on practice	
Impact timeframe	Short-term	Medium-term	Long-term

Adapted from [1].

Information SETA can take on various forms. For example:

- Many universities offer a diploma or degree in Information Security Systems. Although it is recommended that some of the staff in the organization do hold such a degree, e.g., the Information Security Officer, it is definitely not the idea to educate users to such levels.
- Many training courses exist to implement and manage technical Information Security aspects in the organization's systems. Examples are courses on firewalls, intrusion detection, virus control, etc. Again, similar to the above, these courses will be a total over-kill to the average end-user.

Therefore, it is important that Information SETA are done at the correct level of detail to ensure that all end-users are empowered to do their individual jobs more securely.

From the table above, it can be deduced that only Information Security awareness might not be enough. By merely being aware of some information-related threats or controls, one does not necessarily know how to circumvent it (training) and, therefore, one might fail in doing so. Further, if one is aware of some security controls that need to be followed and one has the necessary skills (through training) to do so, but one does not understand why one has to do so (lack of education), then one might look for ways and means to side-step these controls.

One of the main reasons why such SETA programmes fail is because too much technical detail is included in the content; therefore, they must be offered at the correct level of technical detail. Including too much technical detail is a sure route to an unsuccessful SETA programme.

The objective of any SETA programme should be to empower each employee to do his/her job securely and not to turn all employees into security experts.

Whether called Information Security Education, Training and Awareness or merely Information Security Awareness, it is important that employees are taught how to follow the prescribed procedures (training) and why they have to follow it (education), otherwise employees might not be successful in doing their jobs securely.

10.5 The Conscious Competence Learning Model

The Conscious Competence Learning Model [2] lists four stages through which learning takes place. These stages are:

Stage 1: Unconscious Incompetent

At first a person does not realize that he/she does not know how to do certain things and is, therefore, unconscious incompetent.

At first, it is important to make the individual aware that he/she is incompetent as far as that specific task is concerned.

Therefore, most employees are at first unconsciously incompetent as far as Information Security is concerned and some Information Security awareness exercise should be undertaken to make the employee aware that he/she is incompetent to adequately perform his/her job securely.

Stage 2: Conscious Incompetent

Having made the employee aware that he/she is incompetent to do his/her job securely, the employee is now consciously incompetent. Therefore, it is important that the employee is trained to do his/her job in a secure manner.

Stage 3: Conscious Competence

Having mastered the necessary skills to conduct a job in a secure way, the employee can be seen as being consciously competent.

Thus, the employee knows what to do and how to do it to ensure his/her job is done in a secure manner, but the employee stays conscious of it and still needs to concentrate in order to perform the necessary procedures correctly.

Stage 4: Unconscious Competence

At this stage the employee knows that his/her needs to do their job in a secure manner. The employee has also mastered the necessary skills to do so, but still needs to concentrate on following the necessary procedures and practices.

The objective is now, through enough practice and experience, for the employee to make all Information Security-related practices and skills inherent to his/her normal daily actions and behaviour In this way the employee will not think about doing his/her job securely, but it will be part of his/her natural behaviour.

To instill an unconsciously competent behaviour in all employees will ensure that employees inherently perform their jobs in a secure manner. This is sometimes referred to as one of the steps to cultivating an Information Security culture in an organization.

To eventually cultivate an Information Security culture in the organization should be the ultimate objective of management.

It should be noted that SETA will certainly assist to reduce Information Security-related incidents, BUT only those incidents related to employee incompetence and negligence. Information Security-related incidents that result from malicious intent will not necessarily be reduced.

10.6 Approaches used in Information Security Awareness

As mentioned earlier, whether it is called an Information Security Awareness Programme or an Information Security Education, Training and Awareness Programme, elements of education, training and awareness need to be present. The rest of this chapter will refer to Information Security Awareness, which includes relevant elements of education and training as well.

- Training sessions

  Most Information Security Awareness programmes do include some formal sessions or workshops. During such sessions presentations are done educating the audience about aspects such as:

  - Why information is such an important asset?
  - The information security policy and procedures
  - The role and responsibility of every employee
  - The consequences of not complying with the policy

  Having 'educated' the audience on topics like those mentioned above, it is important to train them with regard to their individual actions and behaviour when working with company information. Such training should typically address issues such as:

  - User identification and authentication (passwords)
  - How to choose a password
  - No sharing of user IDs and passwords, etc.
  - Virus control
  - Backing-up information
  - Sharing and storing confidential information
  - Secure email usage
  - Secure Internet usage
  - Social engineering
  - Handling of mobile devices, e.g., notebooks and PDAs
  - Legal usage of software
  - Office manners and discipline, e.g., clean desk
  - Required actions if a security incident or breach is suspected.

Once this training session has been done, employees should know why and how to perform their jobs securely.

Example:

The following is a typical example of how an Information Security Awareness course can be structured and prepared:

There are seven modules, each presented as separate topics;

  - Security in General
  - Information Security in Perspective
  - Password
  - Viruses
  - Data Storage and Backup
  - Computer Ethics
  - Office Discipline.

The following are typical presentation slides that can be used to offer the module on *passwords*.

Passwords, your unique identification to the electronic world.

The objective of any password system is to uniquely identify every user.

Passwords
What is a password?

What are User IDs and Passwords?
▸   **User ID identifies an individual**
        Example: A passport

In any computer system, every user is issued with a user ID and a password.

The user ID identifies the user to the system, like a passport or an ID book.

Passwords
What is a password?

What are User IDs and Passwords?
▸   User ID identifies an individual
        Example: A passport
▸   **User password authenticates a user**
        Example: Signature

The password authenticates the user. This means it proves that the user is indeed who he or she claims to be.

The password is like a signature or fingerprint.

Passwords
Keep it secret!!!!

If another user knows your password;
    Transactions can be done on your behalf

The user ID is usually not kept secret, but it is very important that your password should always be kept absolutely confidential.

If your password is compromised, somebody else can act on your behalf and, for example, do transactions under your name.

Passwords
Keep it secret!!!!
 	
If another user knows your password;
   › Transactions can be done on your behalf
   › **You might be held responsible**
 	
NEVER let anyone get
hold of your password
	In such a case, YOU might be held responsible for such unauthorized transactions.
	
	Thus, to protect yourself, and your organization, it is imperative that your password is never compromised.

Passwords Choosing a password When choosing a password, do not use: › **First or last names** *Joe Soap*	Because your password is so important, it is essential that you choose a password that would not easily be guessed. The following are some guidelines to choosing a proper, secure password. Firstly, never choose first or last names.

Passwords
Choosing a password
 	
When choosing a password, do not use:
   › First or last names
   › **User ID**
	Do not use a password that is similar to your user ID.

Passwords
Choosing a password
 	
When choosing a password, do not use:
   › First or last names
   › User ID
   › **Dictionary words**
	Any word that can be located in a dictionary should be avoided.

Passwords Choosing a password When choosing a password, do not use: › First or last names › User ID › Dictionary words › **Acronyms**	Acronyms, like BBC, UNESCO, etc should not be used.
Passwords Choosing a password When choosing a password, do not use: › First or last names › User ID › Dictionary words › Acronyms › **Geographical words**	Names of geographical locations, such as Alaska, Africa, France, etc, are also not good options.
Passwords Choosing a password When choosing a password, do not use: › First or last names › User ID › Dictionary words › Acronyms › Geographical words › **Addresses**	Any reference to any address, specifically your own, should be avoided. Stay away from street, neighborhood, or city names. They can easily be guessed
Passwords Choosing a password When choosing a password, do not use: › First or last names › User ID › Dictionary words › Acronyms › Geographical words › Addresses › **Fictional characters** Babe	Fictional characters like Babe, Garfield, Mickey, Pluto and so on are generally used because they can easily be remembered. But they are bad choices as passwords. Thus, any words that can be searched for or looked-up anywhere are bad choices as passwords.

Passwords Choosing a password Guidelines in choosing a password: › **Minimum 6 characters** sgtjuk	Proper passwords should be at least six characters long.
Passwords Choosing a password Guidelines in choosing a password: › Minimum 6 characters › **Combination of digits, alphabetic and special characters** sg+tj9	It should ideally include a combination of digits, alphabetic and special characters.
Passwords Choosing a password Guidelines in choosing a password: › Minimum 6 characters › Combination of digits, alphabetic and special characters › **Mixed upper and lower case characters** Rg+tJ9	Upper and lower-case characters should be used.
Passwords Choosing a password Guidelines in choosing a password: › Minimum 6 characters › Combination of digits, alphabetic and special characters › Mixed upper and lower case characters › **Choose a sentence and string words together** Example: Mary had a little lamb 25 Dec Mhall25D →	A good idea is to take an easy-to-remember sentence and choose the first character of every word. This should provide a strong password that is easily remembered.
Passwords Important *Remember, your password is your fingerprint or signature. Somebody else might misuse it, leaving you responsible!*	Your password is very important. Would you give signing rights to your bank account to other people, someone you barely know or trust? If not, for the same reasons, do NOT let other people get hold of your password. YOU will be on the receiving end.

- Information Security Website

  Many organizations do have an Information Security website on their Intranet. The following are typical services and information found on such a website:

  - This website might offer the abovementioned training course electronically for the employees to study in their own time;
  - Names and contact details to report an incident;
  - Tips and guidelines.

  If such a website can be used effectively and employees can be motivated to visit it regularly, it can be very effective.

- Videos

  Training videos can also be used with great effect to educate employees.

  If all of the above education and training possibilities can be done in close cooperation with the HR department, the results can be very successful, especially, during the induction programme of new employees.

  Many organizations do not issue a newly appointed employee with a user ID and password until the initial Information Security training session has been completed successfully.

  Once employees have been educated and trained on *why* they should protect information and *how* to do so, it is important to keep employees aware and alert. For this reason, continuous reminders should take place in various ways. The following are some of the ways and means that can be used to keep everybody aware and alert.

- Information Security Day

  The idea of an annual Information Security Day is very common nowadays. Many organizations use such a day to remind all employees that Information Security is everybody's responsibility and that every colleague may be a possible imposter.

  During such an Information Security Day high visibility is given to security issues. Many employees wear t-shirts with appropriate messages on them, posters are placed in prominent places, flyers are distributed, competitions are run with security as a theme, users are given key-rings with a message on them, etc.

- Regular Communication to Employees

  It is important that regular communication takes place to all end-users to keep them alert. The following media can be used for this purpose:

  - Regular emails, e.g., a security tip for the week;
  - A column in the company newspaper;
  - An Information Security newspaper.

  The typical contents that can be communicated to users using the abovementioned media are:

- o Security tips;
- o Security statistics;
- o New security threats;
- o Security incidents.

No matter what media is used, it is important to keep all information users alert. One must be careful though, that one does not flood users with too many security tips, stats, facts, etc. This might, in fact, have the opposite effect.

- Security Posters, Brochures, Mouse Pads and Magnets

Any possible means should be used to assist in making and keeping information users aware of the imminent security threats and what their roles and responsibilities are as far as that is concerned.

The following *mouse pad* can be used to serve multiple purposes. It:

- o records and reminds the individual of some commitment made;
- o does remind the individual of some critical information;
- o does have contact numbers of the Help Desk and Information Security Officer at hand.

Certificate
Information Security Awareness

This serves to certify that I,   Joe Soap   have successfully completed the ???????? Information Security Awareness Programme and that I undertake:

Passwords

To choose a difficult to guess password
To change my passwords regularly
Not to share my passwords with anyone
Not to write any of my passwords down

Office Discipline

To sign off or lock computer when not near it
To keep my desk clean of sensitive information
To be alert for information security breaches
Not to misuse the company computer system

Data Back-up

To regularly make back-ups of critical files on my PC
To regularly save the work I'm busy with

Viruses

To ensure that the virus control on my PC is active
Not to open any suspicious files

I will always be alert to possible information security breaches and will immediately report any suspicious security events to the ????????? Help Desk at XXXX or the Information Security Officer at ????.

Trust me – I will protect ???????'s valuable information to the best of my ability

10.7 Summary

As more and more employees in any organization work with company information, it becomes increasingly important that all of these users actively participate in protecting organizational information effectively. Information Security can no longer be protected through physical and technical means alone. The human operational aspect has become very important.

For this reason, it is important that all employees are educated, trained and continuously made aware of their responsibility in this regard. Information Security Awareness is a continuous task and drivers of such awareness programmes should never stop thinking of new innovative ways and means to keep all information users aware and alert.

In the next, and last chapter, everything covered in this book is consolidated in a practical methodology.

References

1. Whitman, ME, Mattord, HJ (2003) Principles of Information Security, Thomson Course Technology, Boston
2. Chapman, A. Conscious Competence Learning Model. Available from http://www.businessballs.com/consciouscompetencelearningmodel.htm. Accessed 13 April 2007

Chapter 11
A Methodology for Establishing an Information Security Governance Environment

11.1 Introduction

The previous chapters examined some of the major components of our Information Security Governance Model. There should now be a good understanding of the different dimensions (components) discussed in these chapters.

The question now is:

How do we put it all together, i.e., how do we go about establishing an environment based on the content of this book?

This chapter will provide a high-level methodology on how to establish an ISG environment. The methodology will consist of a number of setup steps followed by a continuous cycle, which can be followed to get such an environment operational.

Our methodology will assume that no such environment exists at all, and that everything must be started from scratch. That is, of course, unrealistic. In most cases, some type of Information Security management environment will already exist, and we should re-use as much as possible to prevent wasting unnecessary time and money. Therefore, the present situation must be compared with the steps provided in the methodology, and must be synchronized and integrated where possible.

There are 14 steps included in the methodology, but that can be refined as needed. The first nine are setup steps, while the last five form a continuous cycle.

11.2 The Steps in the Methodology

The 14 steps in the Framework are listed below and then discussed briefly.

Step 1: Get the Board's buy-in about IT Risk Management and Information Protection
Step 2: Select some guiding Best Practices
Step 3: Perform a basic Risk Analysis and determine all controls needed

S.H. von Solms, R. von Solms, *Information Security Governance*,
DOI 10.1007/978-0-387-79984-1_11, © Springer Science+Business Media, LLC 2009

Step 4: Create a Corporate Information Security Policy (CISP) and get the CISP signed by the Chairman/CEO

Step 5: Create the rest of the Information Security Policy Architecture (ISPA)

Step 6: Create an organizational structure for Information Security Governance (ISG)

Step 7: Create an initial set of Compliance/Control measures and start using these measures to create reports on all three management levels

Step 8: Create and implement an Awareness Programme including aspects like Information Security job responsibilities

Step 9: Get the cycle going – kickstart the process

Step 10: Redo the Risk Analysis from time to time to identify the possible changes in risks and controls

Step 11: Keep the Information Security Policy Architecture up to date and in line with newly identified risks

Step 12: Refine and expand the Compliance Control measures to cater for newly identified risks, enforce compliance and keep reporting to top management

Step 13: Continue to make all users more Information Security aware

Step 14: Return to Step 10

Step 1: Get the Board'sbuy-in about IT Risk Management and Information Protection

This is a very important staring point. Without such buy-in, the project will surely have problems in progressing properly. Initially it may not be possible to get the type of Board Directive as provided in Chapter 6, but that is not essential. As long as there is a commitment from the Board to support the project, that is enough to start. The formal Board Directive can come later – but be sure to get it!

Use the content of Chapters 1, 2 and 3 to make a case to the Board.

Step 2: Select some guiding Best Practices

As discussed in Chapter 5, it is very good to choose some existing international Best Practice to use as a foundation for the project, and to provide motivation and direction.

As discussed, ISO 27002 and COBIT are good candidates, but any other suitable one may be selected. The essential aspect is to have one. Use Chapter 4 as part of the motivation of why such a guiding Best Practice is important.

Step 3: Perform a basic Risk Analysis and determine all controls needed

As we have seen in several chapters, but specifically Chapter 8, it is important to perform some type of Risk Analysis. If it is not precisely clear what the company's electronic assets are, and against what threats these assets must be protected, the chances are that money will be spent on countermeasures which are not necessarily the correct ones.

In this exercise it is essential to get a wide spectrum of people involved – Board members, line management, users, system owners etc. This will ensure buy-in to the results from a wide group of stakeholders.

Chapter 8, as well as the approach in Paragraph 7.8, does provide some guidance on how to approach such a Risk Analysis exercise.

Ensure that the relevant controls are installed and operational.

Step 4: Create a Corporate Information Security Policy (CISP) and get the CISP signed by the Chairman/CEO

After the Risk Analysis exercise of Step 3, buy-in from all relevant stakeholders should be forthcoming. A CISP must now be drafted, using the guidelines given in Chapter 6. This draft document must be circulated amongst the stakeholders mentioned above, and then submitted to top management. It is essential that by this point in time a more formal Board Directive on Information Security had been provided from top management. As suggested in Chapter 6, this Directive should be used as the driver for the CISP.

To get the CISP signed by the Chairman/CEO is crucial to the whole exercise. If a Board Directive is available at this point, the step will be much easier because the two documents are related. The Draft CISP must now be signed and made official company policy. This will now provide the basis and motivation for all future steps.

Step 5: Create the rest of the Information Security Policy Architecture (ISPA)

Using Chapter 6 as a guide, create the ISPA.

Note: Steps 1–5 above must basically be done sequentially. Steps 6–8 can be done in parallel.

Step 6: Create the organizational structure for ISG

With the background of Chapter 9, create or restructure the ISG structure of the company. Specific attention must be given to the Operational Management and Compliance Management sides. This step is closely related to Step 7, so they will probably be done in parallel.

Step 7: Create an initial set of Compliance/Control measures and start using these measures to create reports on all three management levels

As discussed in Chapter 9, this aspect is very important. In this step, it is important to get buy-in from the company's Internal and External IT Auditor departments as well as the Legal department. If these were involved in Step 3 above, this process will be much easier. As discussed in Chapter 9, creating such measures is not straightforward, and the effectiveness and value of such measures will have to be refined over time. It is, however, important to start off with an initial set of measures which will form the basis of the 'Control' part of the model discussed in Chapter 5.

Step 8: Create an Awareness Programme including aspects like information security job responsibilities

Chapter 10 should provide the background here. As stated, this step is core to the success of the whole effort, and must be performed on a continuous basis. All the documents in the ISPA should form part of the Awareness Programme.

Step 9: Get the cycle going – kick start the process

At this point the whole programme must be initiated, or if one already exists, the revised one must be integrated with the existing one to get the new one operational.

Step 10: Redo the Risk Analysis from time to time to identify the possible changes in risks and controls

IT risks, like all other types of risks, are dynamic – old ones go away, new ones materialize and existing ones change their impact. It is, therefore, important to redo any Risk Analysis from time to time to ensure that the risk situation is up to date and that relevant controls are installed and operational.

Step 11: Keep the ISPA up to date and in line with newly identified risks

Ensure that all changed risks are reflected in the ISPA by changing the content of the ISPA and Compliance Clauses, if necessary.

Step 12: Refine and expand the Compliance Control measures to cater for newly identified risks, enforce compliance and keep reporting to top management

As stated in Chapter 7, the choice and creation of Compliance Clauses and Compliance Monitoring measures are not easy, and stay a challenging process. Therefore, the process never stops, and experience is continuously gathered, which must be used to refine these measures and create new ones. It is, however, essential to use whatever measures are available, right from the start, to enforce compliance and to create reporting structures.

Step 13: Continue to make all users more Information Security Aware

This process can never stop, and must be enforced on a continuous basis.

Step 14: Return to Step 10.

11.3 Summary

By integrating all the chapters of this book, and being guided by the methodology provided above, it should be possible to create an Information Security Governance Framework for any company.

Index

Note: The letters '*f*' and '*t*' following the locators refer to figures and tables respectively